Celtic

DAILY LIFE

Celtic
DAILY LIFE

INCLUDING
herb lore ✛ *metalwork* ✛ *wine and brewing*
feasts ✛ *recipes* ✛ *clothing* ✛ *perfume*
marriage rites ✛ *legends and beliefs*

VICTOR WALKLEY

Book-of-the-Month Club
New York

This book is dedicated to
Jocelyne, my wife, who died December 18, 1995
and to the Anglo-Celtic Fraternal Alliance

Contents

Introduction

Preparation of this book has taken a period of some fifty years, but its real beginning was well before that time. It may have commenced at that moment when, during school holidays, I rambled across the hills with my school friends. We came across a mound and a circular ditch, which was later identified as an Iron Age fort. Of course, this became the backdrop to our well-rehearsed games. It was the castle of the Saxons fighting the Vikings, or the stronghold of King Arthur. We spent our weekends and holidays roaming the hills and forests that surrounded our home.

We wandered far, often until darkness fell, and sometimes even spent the night in a cave at the foot of the cliff, a cave that may have been used by our ancestors 3,000 years ago. We took apples, bread and cheese, potatoes to roast in the hot embers of the campfire and a screw of tea, which we brewed in an old tin can with water from the hill stream. At nightfall we watched the flittering bats, outlined against the moon, and listened with bated breath as the screech owls disturbed our sleep, or a stone dislodged by some night animal rattled down from the cliff. We told each other stories we had heard from our grandparents, or from the story-

teller—tales of warriors and battles in distant ages. And we crowded closer to the fire when we retold stories of the gods and demons that inhabited the burial mounds. When the grey mist enshrouded the hill, we became wrapped in a cocoon of mystery, and we knew that the little people of the moor and the goblins of the forest were holding their revels, as they had done for a thousand ages past.

When a team of archaeologists came to make a dig at the place we knew as "the moat", we watched them secretly from our hide-out among the trees; when they left the site at evening, we crept out to see what progress they had made. With all the assurance of youth, we children thought we knew more about the ancient history of the place than any book-learned academic. We did not tell them of the place where hundreds of carved stones lay hidden in the undergrowth. Or of the grave-mound that covered the body of a Celtic chief, with sword, chariot and armour of gold, who walked the earth at Samhain when the long-dead warriors rose from the clay of their tombs.

Some compelling spirit of curiosity drove me to seek more facts about our Celtic ancestors. I listened to tales of wonder and enchantment, news from people who lived in these remote places and legends handed down from their fore-

bears. The church, built of weathered stone from the nearby quarry, gave me no information. The saints and martyrs, entombed in their stained-glass windows, looked down with sightless eyes on an uncomprehending congregation. Words from the pulpit froze my imagination—redemption, hell and everlasting fire. Tombstones, half eroded by time, lichen-covered, grey and stark, marked occupants awaiting resurrection from their bed of earth at the last trumpet blast. The church bell sang its rule of prayer and pealed the chimes, stripping away the flesh of time from life. None answered the questions that I asked.

At school, chalk scraped on smooth slate as we learned the "three R's", a little history and geography, and attended assembly and hymn singing. I awaited revelation, hoping to learn something of our ancestors, their way of life, their crafts and skills, but no enlightenment came. Then came the school bell—signalling the headlong rush for freedom and the high hill and the secret cave where sword blade rang against shield and helm.

Fortunately, my paternal grandfather possessed a great horde of books: five rooms with overflowing bookshelves and centre aisles of shelves reaching to the ceiling. No one was allowed in grandfather's kingdom of books except for

Alice, who dusted, tended the fire and brought coal, and myself. From a very early age, I was allowed access, and it was here I learned to read. There were books on theology that I wondered at and understood only years later; books on history, Shakespeare, Milton, early Bibles, books on science, astronomy and the arts. There were cupboards and drawers full of fascinating artefacts that I dared only to touch, including a Celtic sword hilt, earthenware oil lamps and a silver chalice—did this once hold the blood of Christ, the Holy Grail of ancient legend? When the sky was grey, and wind-blown rain darkened the landscape, Grandfather would read to me. Sometimes he recited legends of the Celtic Fianna and the Mabinogion, the mythical tales of Cuchulain and Finn McCool, stories of the Children of Lir and of Usna.

My early holidays with my cousin in the Forest of Dean brought me into contact with the charcoal burners, men who were almost a race apart. I was able to watch them at work, and when I returned home I made a small-scale unit and, using similar methods, produced a quantity of willow charcoal of quite respectable quality. Encouraged at this success, I carefully read *The Boy's Playbook of Science*, published in 1864, and managed to produce coal gas from coal and to etch metals with acid.

Celtic Daily Life

The iron-ore mines in the Forest of Dean (locally called scowl-holes) had been worked since Celtic times. I explored those deep cuttings and scrambled along the passageways, hopeful that I might catch a glimpse of those early miners. I took back with me a quantity of iron ore which I attempted to refine, without success. Similarly, a visit to Cornwall showed me mines where tin ore had been extracted since Phoenician times. This gave me an insight into the antiquity of some mining and refining practices that the Celts would have used in producing metals and alloys.

During the Second World War, I joined the Royal West African Frontier Force, training men in the Gold Coast (now Ghana) and Nigeria. Eventually, we were sent to India, and later, Burma, where we stayed after war's end, working in civil administration. During the course of my travels, I was fortunate to be able to study local craftsmen at work. It was evident that many of their techniques and skills, though often described as "primitive", were very effective. These same methods had been used by other civilisations in the past, including those of the Celtic people. The refining of ores, the forging of metal and preparation of alloys, pottery and artwork, all had similarity to Celtic practice. So did the tanning of hides and skins; the construction of river

craft from fallen timber; building of wooden and thatched huts, dams and irrigation channels; and rustic methods of agriculture using both draught animals (water buffalo) and manual means. I also observed the polishing and setting of precious and semi-precious stones, manufacture of metalware and decorative objects, wood carving and metal engraving, and the fabrication of tools and implements at the blacksmith's forge. Although these operations were carried out with the most rudimentary equipment, they were done precisely and at amazing speed.

On my return to the UK in 1947, I took a position as microbiologist and chief chemist with a company of distillers, who produced whisky in Scotland, gin in London and also had an extensive wine business. All of these manufacturing processes were applicable to Celtic practice. Later I became their technical director, and managing director of a company I had set up within the group, which dealt primarily with essences and essential oils. I also served on the board of an international company with extensive business in Europe and the Mediterranean region.

As the company had factories in both Britain and Ireland, I lived for some time in Northern Ireland, Eire and Scotland, and came into contact with what is described by some as

"the Celtic fringe", people who retain much of their ancestors' ancient tradition, beliefs and culture.

At this time I had quite a large laboratory set up at my home, and with extensive ground space and outhouses, was able to carry out such experiments as tanning skins and hides, leathermaking, manufacturing ointments and medicinal preparations from herbs, and brewing Celtic beer (*korma*) and mead—all with materials and methods used by Celtic craftsmen.

My long overseas business trips took me all over Europe and the Mediterranean region. Thus I continued my study of various rural crafts and learned local methods to produce soaps, ointments, medical products, and cosmetics and perfumes from herbs, flowers, roots and oils. I lived for some years in Arabia, where the Badawa people taught me how they used herbs and plants to make dyes for wool and animal hair. On holidays in India and North Africa, often accompanied by my late wife, Jocelyne, I continued my studies. My notebook was gradually progressing toward a manuscript. We also visited Celtic monastic and settlement sites in Britain and Ireland and studied in museums. Ongoing field trials and bench experiments helped to establish the accuracy of records of ancient techniques.

INTRODUCTION

All of these experiences have contributed to this book, which I hope will interest many readers in our rich Celtic heritage, focussing on the simple day-to-day activities of homestead and workshop, ritual and beliefs, and living closely with nature. It concerns a diverse but valorous people, sometimes warlike, but demonstrating compassion and a love of life that set them apart from the barbarian tribes that surrounded them. We of these islands have been spared most of the influences that destroyed the Celtic ideal elsewhere. Thus we are the only people who possess this inheritance almost intact, and who can help to preserve it for future generations. ⊕ ⊕ ⊕

VICTOR WALKLEY
1997

THE CELTIC
PEOPLE

Who Were the Celts?

A diverse and widespread people, from Asia Minor to the British Isles, the ancient Celts left a lasting imprint on the evolution of European society, particularly in Scotland, Wales and Ireland, where Celtic tradition, legend and lore are still evident today. For those whose curiosity is piqued, there are pointers as to how the people of this magnificent civilisation lived. Nebulous and half-glimpsed, for the most part, these pointers help us to form a living picture of the Bronze Age Celts of the British Isles and their successors.

It is impossible to define precisely the period when the Celts emerged as a cultural entity upon the world stage, but several threads of continuity link them with their origins. We can trace them back to the first millennium BC, and by 500 BC they had already formed large communities in Europe. Hecateus of Miletus, who wrote c. 500 BC, notes that Narbonne was a Celtic town, and that Celtic territory bordered on Massalia (modern Marseilles, France), which was then a Greek outpost. A few years later, Herodotus mentions that Celts were living on the Upper Danube, near the Pyrenees and in Spain. The Greek soldier and historian Xenophon refers to Celtic mercenary soldiers who were

hired by Dionysius the Elder of Syracuse; they fought against the Thebans in the Peloponnesos in 369 BC.

By the early fourth century BC, the Celtic migration was well under way, as tribes moved west from their ancestral homes on the Rhine and Danube. They crossed the Alps into Italy, occupied the valley of the Po, and plundered Rome in 390 BC, taking tribute from the imperial city. Some warriors raided Apulia and ranged as far south as Sicily. Other tribes made raids into Illyria, on the Adriatic coast, and into Pannonia and the Carpathians. In 279 BC, Celts occupied and laid waste to Macedonia and Thrace, then invaded Greece, where they plundered the temple at Delphi. For centuries they would terrorise Greek colonial cities.

Archaeological excavation of Celtic towns and villages in Europe, and grave findings from the early era, show clearly that the Celts enjoyed a secure and prosperous life. Grave goods frequently include richly decorated spears and shields, gold neck rings (torques), helmets, metal and pottery vessels, toilet implements, drinking horns and cauldrons. Women's graves provide even more magnificent pieces: brooches and earrings, elaborate collars and corsets, engraved bronze mirrors, beads and rings—all exquisite items decorated profusely in the Celtic style. From these sources,

and from votive offerings found in pools and pits, we can construct a reliable picture of their art and artefacts and their love of personal adornment.

Certain Celtic tribes migrated north from Gaul and populated much of Britain. Other migrants from Western Europe and Iberia made their homes in Ireland and, later, Scotland. It is probable that the first Celts to arrive in Britain were traders, followed later by families, until the time when whole tribes made the British Isles their permanent home. Movement of the larger tribes was due primarily to the overpopulation of Gaul, but the subsequent Roman invasion of Europe was also a major factor. Certainly, the southern part of Britain offered the right climate and extensive areas of land ideally suited to the cultivation of grain and the raising of cattle, sheep and ponies. Another attraction was mineral ore—particularly iron and tin—accessible to mining. Huge forests provided fuel for smelting the ore. ⊕ ⊕ ⊕

ḣistorical Records of the Celts

We have learned much about the Celts from the accounts of classical writers. Of the early writers who commented upon Celtic affairs, the Stoic philosopher Posodonius, who lived in the first century BC, is probably the most reliable. Many later geographers and historians, including Julius Caesar, relied on Posodonius for their information. Unfortunately, only a few fragments of his works remain, and we must now refer to three later Greek writers—Diodorus Sicula, Strabo and Athenaeus—for much of our information.

We must be cautious, however, in placing too much emphasis on these sources. Most of the classical authors were inimical to the Celts, whom they considered bloodthirsty barbarians. Nevertheless, it was the Celts' ability as farmers, artisans, craftsmen and traders that supported their economy and stabilised their society. Indeed, it was their growing wealth and economic power that created envy and fear in Rome, leading eventually to the Roman invasion of Celtic Europe. Greek and Roman interpretations of Celtic affairs were coloured by political and socio-economic biases. The Greeks knew them as *keltoi*, the Romans as *Galli*—and both saw them as a threat to their economic and social structures.

Diodorus Sicula stated that "the Britons live in the same manner as the ancients did: they fight in chariots, as the ancient heroes of Greece are said to have done in the Trojan Wars....They are plain and upright in their dealings, and far from the craft and subtlety of our countrymen". Of their hospitality, he reports: "The Celts never shut the doors of their houses; they invite strangers to their feasts, and when it is all over, ask who they are and what is their business".

Other ancient writers, including Dion Cassius and Strabo, provide vivid descriptions and biographical information on such notable figures as the renowned queen of the Iceni, Boudicca, who is remembered as the champion of her people's rights. "Her stature exceeded the ordinary height of women; her aspect was calm and collected, but her voice had become deep and pitiless. Her hair, falling in long tresses as low as her hips, was collected round her forehead by a golden coronet; she wore a striped dress fitting closely to the bosom, but below the waist expanding in loose folds as a gown; over it was a chlamys or military cloak. In her hand she bore a spear".

Pliny the Younger, the Roman writer and historian who perished in the eruption of Vesuvius in AD 79, had lived for some time among the Celts and knew them well. His writ-

ings include quite detailed records of aspects of their daily life, such as his description of the special soap prepared by women to enhance their complexions.

Neither Greek nor Roman literati comment on the ability of the Celts to speak languages other than their own, but the Celts were accomplished linguists. Their trading activities brought them into contact with many civilisations. In addition to Greek and early Latin, some would have spoken Syriac (Aramaic) and the languages of eastern Europe. The Celtic language has correspondences with the Italic of ancient Italy and has been subdivided for semantic purposes into Gaulish (obsolete); Goidelic, which includes Scottish Gaelic, Irish and Manx; and Brythonic, including Welsh, Breton and Cornish (the latter now in process of revival). Pictish is related to Brythonic Welsh.

Although the early Celts were not literate, they had remarkable memories and passed on their history and traditions orally. Caesar remarked on the outstanding memory of the Gauls, and several of their orators were highly esteemed. From the first century AD, Gaulish tutors were employed for the sons of eminent Roman families, and the recall and skill of the Gaelic storyteller would become a byword. Other written clues are scant: place names, for example, have

helped yield information about the Celts. It was not until about the fifth century AD that Celtic authors routinely recorded their history, faith and beliefs in their own beautifully illuminated manuscripts. ⊕ ⊕ ⊕

Celtic Society

Classical accounts of the Celts vary widely, but all the historians emphasised that Celtic society was stratified, with a ruling warrior class. The warrior aristocracy obtained their wealth not only from refining and working metals—especially iron—but from cultivation and their relatively advanced knowledge of animal husbandry. Only the priests were accorded a higher status than this wealthy class.

The Celtic warriors were feared throughout Europe. Describing the battle of Telamon in 255 BC, Polybius wrote of the Celtic military élite: "Very terrifying were the appearance and gestures of the naked warriors in front, all in the prime of life and finely built men, and all in the leading companies richly adorned with gold torques and armlets". Women, too, were feared in battle. "A whole band of foreigners will be unable to cope with one of them in a fight,

if he calls for his wife, stronger than he by far and with flashing eyes; least of all when she swells her neck and gnashes her teeth, and poising her huge white arms, begins to rain blows mingled with kicks like shots discharged by the twisted cord of a catapult", observed one Roman writer.

We know that slave labour was a feature of Celtic life. One Greek author mentions that the Celt would barter a slave for a jar of wine, a servant for a drink. Another source details that "six heifers equals three milch cows, equals one female slave". Slaves were exported from the British Isles, and there are good grounds to suppose that some were imported, or taken captive in distant countries and brought back as spoils of war. Some were employed as domestics and for child care, while others laboured on the farm and in mines and construction, or assisted craftsmen. There are also records of slaves who travelled with their masters and mistresses to act as translators and assist with foreign trading and business.

The exact position of slaves in Celtic society is obscure. They could own land and have rights to inherit land and other property under certain conditions. They were, how-ever, themselves the property of the *tuath* (kindred), and free tribesmen would have extra slaves accredited to them

at crucial times, such as sowing and harvesting, in the case of farmers. So-called "slave chains", made of iron links and collars, have been found, but these are more likely to have been used for the detention and public parading of prisoners of war than to confine servants and slaves already established in the homestead. It is believed that children born to women slaves and fathered by free tribesmen were accorded *tuath* status. When the chief of a *tuath* died, it was customary to free a number of the family's slaves, a tradition that was also practised in the Roman Empire.

The majority of the written accounts of Celtic life concentrate on warriors and the wealthy. Relatively little was recorded on ordinary lives, yet the strength of the Celtic economy lay in small farming. Throughout the British Isles, there are places where the shapes and patterns of Celtic villages are still visible. Fortified settlements were common. Large areas of good cropping soil were arranged in a network of fields, all linked by tracks. Villages and individual farmsteads were positioned within the area, and very often a fort served as a focus for social assembly. In times of danger, these forts also provided a refuge, both for people and their livestock. The forts were built on hills or, sometimes, on artificial islands that were created by driving wooden

piles into lake beds and filling in the centre with stones. The forts were built of dry stone walls and sometimes had internal wooden structures for support.

Within the fortified village, family dwellings were usually round or rectangular structures built of pegged timbers and roofed with thatch. A hearth, sometimes with a clay oven, was centrally placed in the home, and smoke was vented through the roof. Winter storage of food and animal fodder (usually hay and roots) was communal; the village's walled enclosure was shared.

Much has been written about Roman roads, but there is evidence that equally important roads were built much earlier. Roads, bridges and, in swampy regions, raised causeways were built with the use of slave labour. Wooden roads, constructed up to five thousand years ago, were made out of hazel and ash branches. A built-up road in the Somerset Levels dates to 3700 BC. Unlike Roman roads, which at first were used only by military and state messengers, Celtic roads were used freely by everyone.

In *The Triads of Ireland*, Thomas Kinsella observes that: "There are three things free to a country and its borders: the rivers, the roads and places of worship". Inland waterways were navigated to facilitate transport and supplement

the "green roads" that had existed since Neolithic times. Other routes linked farming communities with trading centres and the sites of fairs and religious shrines.

Within the village, the extended family was the basis of Celtic society. As in most cultures, mealtimes were the focal point of the family's day. The historian Athenaeus provides a vivid description of such a gathering: "The Celts sit on dried grass and have their meals served on wooden tables raised above the ground. Their food consists of a small number of loaves of bread together with a large amount of meat, either boiled or roasted on charcoal or on spits. They partake of this cleanly but in a leonine manner, raising up whole limbs in both hands and biting off the meat, while any part that is hard to tear off, they cut through with a small dagger which hangs attached to their sword-sheath in its own scabbard". ⊕ ⊕ ⊕

Economy, Skills and Trade

A side from farming, the Celts were skilled in many areas, including mining, metalwork, masonry, distilling and weaving. While these skills were used primarily to produce goods for personal use, there was also a great deal of trading, from local bartering to foreign trade for goods not available at home.

Most craft workshops produced for local tastes and demand. Tools and farm implements, clothing and domestic items were traded within small areas. More highly specialised workshops manufactured personal ornaments and decorative items on a much larger scale, and traded them across a wide area. Thus ceremonial chariots, weapons and ornaments of precious metal, including elaborately decorated torques and fibulas, all of which were marketed throughout Britain and Gaul, constituted a large and lucrative export business.

Supporting industries sprang up to meet the demand. Ores were mined and refined. Colour pigments were used for dyeing cloth fabrics and for decorating domestic ware. Farriers shod ponies and oxen with iron shoes, and the smith learned to make such specialised items as surgical

instruments, tweezers and double-blade scissors. Wheels were fitted with iron-hoop rims; the wheelwright made sophisticated bearings and axles. Wagon bodies were detachable, so that they could be placed on sledges drawn by oxen across soft farm fields. Builders and stonemasons, shipbuilders and craftsmen of every calling emerged to support the fast-growing Celtic economy in the British Isles.

It was their mastery of various technical skills and their ability to reform ancient methods of agriculture and stock raising that gave the Celts a unique place in European history. In the art of dyeing wool and linen, for example, they used complex processes to obtain vegetable dyes of a high order. Soaps, cosmetics, body perfumes and lotions were prepared on a cottage-industry scale. Fermentation processes produced both *korma* and vinegar for daily domestic use. Additionally, the Celts imported a wide variety of raw materials from faraway places: lapis lazuli from Badakhshan (in Afghanistan), precious stones from the Indus, silks from China, spices from the Far East. Both the southern Celts and the Picts in the north commanded large merchant fleets, of which Julius Caesar recorded in 52-51 BC that "the hulls were made of oak to sustain any violent shock or impact; the cross-beams, of timber a foot thick, were fastened with

iron bolts as thick as a man's thumb, and the anchors were held firm with iron chains instead of ropes".

Fragments of a document preserved by Festus Aviennus, the *Ora Maritima*, record a journey of exploration to "the outer parts of Europe" by a Phoenician boatmaster, Himlico of Carthage, in the sixth century BC. The document describes the British as "a powerful race, proud-spirited, effectively skilful in art, and constantly busy with the care of trade". As an example, the Celtic hooded cloak was regarded by the Romans as a very superior garment. In Diocletian's *Edict of Prices*, issued in AD 301, the value of the Gallic cloak was the highest on the list. The excellent quality of the wool produced from Celtic flocks and the artistry of the weaving doubtless accounted for its desirability. Martial comments that Britain "for wool [is] past compare".

Strabo comments on the many traders and merchants who carried corn and cattle, iron and hides, to the river ports of the Seine and Rhine, exchanging them for ivory and amber ornaments. We learn from Zosimus that in the reign of Julian (AD 363), 800 pinnaces (small oared sailing vessels) were built in order to ship grain to Gaul. Such was the repute of Celtic craftsmen that many Celts were sent to Rome to teach their skills.

CELTIC DAILY LIFE

In addition to their technical and agricultural skills, the Celts are perhaps most admired for their art, and manuscript art in particular. Celtic art was at first influenced by Iron Age La Tene style. In earlier Celtic-Pictish times, "men of art" were given a high and valued status in society. Those who journeyed among various tribes and across territorial boundaries were given special protection by the High Kings and local rulers. These journeymen included the pattern-makers and, by virtue of their very special knowledge and designwork, they were accepted everywhere. These same craftsmen and pattern-makers travelled between the British Isles and Europe. Some Celtic artists and metalworkers were acquainted with Mediterranean, Syriac and Coptic tradition, and that of Asia Minor and southern Russia. Thus there was a constant intermingling of styles and links with other cultures, but the Celtic art conception was paramount in their own native work.

After the sixth century, the aristocracy and ruling chiefs were no longer the major patrons of the artist and craftsman. The Culdee Church commissioned most works of art, and artist-craftsmen joined monastic communities. Celtic monasteries were as large as towns, and the community employed and organised a considerable number of artisans

to execute major works. From as early as the fourth century AD until the flowering of manuscript work in the tenth and twelfth centuries, monastic institutions produced remarkable and magnificent illuminated work. On vellum and parchment, the monks and chroniclers recorded their history and legends and set down the words of the Gospel. The *Book of Kells*, begun on Iona and finished in Ireland; the *Book of Durrow*; the Lindisfarne Gospels—their beautiful decoration bears the unmistakable imprint of Celtic art. These are a few of what must have been many manuscripts, the majority of them lost to us by warfare, looting and the ravages of time. ⊕ ⊕ ⊕

Religion, Beliefs and Customs

Information on Celtic religion comes to us from a number of different sources, but they must be viewed with caution as no direct evidence is available. It is probable that there were wide differences among the many tribes. We must remember that the Celts owed much to their predecessors. They made use of the megalithic monuments, and although the evidence is tenuous, it poses the question of whether the Druidic order of priests knew to what purpose Stonehenge and other *astro-circles* had been built. The existence of a Druidic priesthood from the beginning of the Celtic race must have meant a continuity of knowledge.

Caesar observed in the *Gallic War* that "the Gallic people as a whole are extremely superstitious", and said of the Druids: "They do not think it right to commit their teaching to writing, although for most other purposes, for example public and private accounts, use the Greek alphabet. I suppose this practice began originally for two reasons: they did not want their doctrines to be accessible to the ordinary people, and they did not want their pupils to rely on the written word and so neglect to train their memories". Druidic beliefs and practices are described in chapter 5, together

with the early Celtic Christian (Culdee) church and widespread superstitions and ceremonial and ritual traditions.

Some information on the pagan Celt is enshrined in myth and story. This is the domain of the ancient storyteller, or *fillid*, who has long since vanished from the scene. There was also interaction between early Celtic Christian beliefs and the ancient faith of the people. Links with ancient Celtic religion appear in traditions and beliefs that are still prevalent in some areas of western Ireland and the Scottish Western Isles. Faith and tradition have the power to influence the daily life of a people, preserving the collective memory.

Many an ancient Celtic story tells us something of their customs. One such tale, the Feast of Briccriu, comes from Ireland. Briccriu Menthenga (Poison-tongue), a larger-than-life Falstaffian character, invites King Conchobar and his warriors to a feast, where he tries to incite Conchobar's heroes to kill one another. Reminding them of the champion's portion—the best cut of meat at the forthcoming feast—he asks slyly, "Who among the men of Ulster is your champion"? Laegaire Buadach, Conall Cernach and Cu Chilainn (or Cuchulain) all claim the *curad-mir*, the champion's portion. They rise to fight, backed by their women. Then they agree to undergo trials, from which Cu Chilainn

emerges the victor. This is a thumbnail sketch of the strict codes that conditioned Celtic social life.

Celtic folklore and legends contain many references to board games, which came after the feast, while the harpists were playing and tales of the Fian were told. In the story "The Love of Etain", Midir contrives to steal back his wife from Eochy, the High King of Ireland. One day Midir appears before the king bearing a silver gameboard, with pieces made of silver and gold. Eochy wins time after time, and Midir performs many tasks as payment. Finally, one last game is played, and Midir asks that the stake be decided by the winner. Eochy agrees, but this time Midir wins the game. In "The Children of Usna", Connor MacNessa, the king of Ulster, seeks revenge upon Naoise, who has robbed him of Deirdre, his bride-to-be. Hoping to regain her, he lures the two back to Ulster by trickery and offers them hospitality in the house of the Red Branch Knights. Then Connor MacNessa sends a warrior to spy on the two lovers, who are engaged in a game of chess. Deirdre, glancing up from the board, sees an eye peering at them through a tiny skylight. She cries out to Naoise to warn him, and he throws one of the chess pieces with such force that it puts out the eye of the spying warrior.

Many of the gods and heroes were highly skilled at board games, and Lugh of the Long Arm is said to have devised a gambit that it still known as Lugh's box. For centuries these stories were memorised and handed down orally, but from the fifth century onward, monks and essayists began to set them down on parchment or paper.

The Celts were visionaries, yet they were also inventive and resourceful. Imagery and romanticism filled their fables and stories, but their intensely practical skills gave them power over their immediate environment. *The Triads of Ireland* give us a glimpse of their spirit:

> *Three things that are always in a decent man's house:*
> *beer, a bath, a good fire.*
> *Three sounds of increase: the lowing of a cow in milk,*
> *the din of a smithy, the kiss of the plough.*
> *Three slendernesses that best hold up the world:*
> *the jet of milk into a pail, the green blade of*
> *corn in the soil, the thread spinning out of a*
> *decent woman's fist.*

OCCUPATIONS
AND SKILLS

farminʒ and Animal husbandry

From about the fourth century BC, the basis of Celtic society was the land. In southeastern Britain, huge forest areas had been cleared and grain was cultivated, both barley of a hardy variety and a form of wheat known as spelt. Thus a barley crop could be sown in the autumn and harvested before the spring-grown spelt, providing two harvests in a single year.

The Celts worked agricultural land by fields, each about an acre in size. Their ploughs were of the straight, iron-shoe type, pulled by one or two oxen. Where necessary, crossploughing was done to break up the soil. The Celtic farm consisted of one or more fields, enclosed and drained where necessary, and a central stockade that housed the domestic quarters, the farm building proper, ancillary barns, husking and winnowing sheds, storage bins and drying racks for hay. There would also be pits or bins to store grain for winter use and as seed stock for the following year. In grassland areas, there were enclosures for livestock and draught animals. Ripe grain was harvested with sickles and a kind of reaping knife.

The first operation after harvesting is to separate the grain from the straw. This was done either by threshing with flails

or by treading under the hooves of draught animals, as is still done in many countries to this day. When large amounts of grain had to be threshed, another method was to use an iron roller, studded with iron knobs. This was drawn across the sheaves, which were spread in a circle along the track of the roller. The grain then had to be winnowed to separate the chaff and grit particles. This was carried out by casting the grain into the air, where the lighter particles of chaff were blown away and the grit and dust separated. This process is still in use, although the "wind" is now derived from motor-driven fans. The grain was ground using a stone saddle quern, which was eventually replaced by the rotary quern, having a flat base and a beehive-shaped upper rotary stone.

Sheep were essential to the Celtic economy, providing milk, meat, wool and valuable by-products including lanolin, used for preparing medicinal salves and body ointments. It was obtained by kneading new-combed sheep's wool in soft water. The natural grease separated and formed an emulsion with the water; when warmed gently, the grease became an oily layer on the surface. This layer was skimmed off, mixed with a new quantity of soft water, mixed gently, and warmed again, then strained through very fine cloth.

The water and oil emulsion was allowed to cool and the clean lanolin, or wool-fat, scooped from the surface.

In the Highlands and Islands of Scotland, peat cutting or "skinning the moss" has been done since time immemorial. Mosses, or peats, cover much of Scotland and Ireland, and for thousands of years turves have been cut, stacked in claves to dry, then carted to homesteads and stored beneath a covering of boughs and heather until needed for fuel. Some of the great peat bogs were once ancient forests, where, over the ages, trees died and fell. Ferns, flowers and grasses took root and flourished in the clearings until new saplings overshadowed them. As the climate grew wetter, trees died out, and beaked sedge, sphagnum moss, cotton grass and other moorland plants took their places. As decaying vegetable matter compacted, the first layers of peat began to form, favoured by the waterlogged conditions that excluded oxygen. In the uplands, from about 5000 BC, peat formed rapidly; in other places, much more slowly. Today there are peat bogs that are thirty feet (ten metres) deep, still serving as a natural source of fuel and a plant covering. Traditional Celtic methods of soil improvement have continued: in some areas, underlying boulder clay is mixed with the surface peat, then seaweeds and other organic matter are added and ploughed

under. In the course of time, this provides excellent agricultural soil. Similarly, crofters in the Outer Hebrides still add tons of shell, sand, animal manure and seaweed in order to recover the land for cultivation. ⊕ ⊕ ⊕

Traders and Currency

As the Celts developed a wider export trade, so their society became economically organised. Those tribes that occupied strategic positions on trade routes devised systems of tolls and taxes, which had to be collected and administered. Some form of policing became necessary. Trade between nations meant that merchants had to pass through territory commanded by various chiefs, mandating a form of trading truce. Armed guards protected the safety of traders and their wares from the bands of outlaws and thieves that would otherwise have overwhelmed them. Internally, organisation of the great trade fairs necessitated active co-operation among local chiefs and rulers.

In addition to their trade in luxury goods, metals, grain and hides, the Celts exchanged other commodities with their neighbours. One of the items most in demand was salt, known

as *salaan*. It was either mined or obtained by the evaporation of sea water in pans. Salt was needed not only for culinary purposes, but for many manufacturing processes. Alum for dyeing and leather making was imported to the British Isles from the Island of Melos in the Aegean Sea.

The earliest Celtic coinage appeared about the second century BC. It was introduced mainly for the trade in grain and hides between Britain and Gaul. Gold coins of the Iceni and Dobunni (30 BC to AD 10) have been found, and silver coins minted locally by the Coritani, Dobunni and Durotriges were discovered in archaeological digs in southern Britain.

The composition and intrinsic worth of Celtic coinage far exceeded the value of modern currencies. If you are fortunate enough to see a Celtic gold coin minted sometime in the second century BC, it will contain between 90 and 97 percent gold. ⊕ ⊕ ⊕

Mining and Metalworking

It is impossible to assess the Celts without relating their accomplishments to those of other people of their time. It has been said that iron was the very lifeblood of the Celt. Not only did it give their warriors superiority in battle, it enabled their farmers to till the soil and reap harvests far in excess of those cultivated by other tribes. Their ability to master complex chemical reactions in many forms of metallurgy was instrumental in making them the envy of Greece and Rome. The British Isles were rich in natural metal deposits, including iron ore, gold, silver, tin and copper. Where certain ores were in short supply locally, they could be imported in exchange for finished goods. Valuable alloys including bronze (made of copper and tin) were improved and made suitable for new applications.

The Celts extracted iron ore in the Forest of Dean, the Weald and along the Jurassic limestone crop from Oxfordshire to Lincolnshire. The Picts produced good quality metal in Scotland, and, reportedly, the Silures and Ordovices Celts of Wales were the most skillful ironworkers of them all. Both iron and its associated minerals were fashioned into many forms of ornamental metalwork.

The ore found in the Forest of Dean and South Wales occurs chiefly as limonite—kidney-shaped masses of ferric oxide (haematite). Other ores include clay ironstone; the brown haematite of Northamptonshire, black band ironstone and the bog iron ore found in Ireland and part of Scotland. After the Roman invasion of Britain, Celtic iron mines and smelters were operated under direct military supervision. Imperial control was also exercised over the Dolocauthi gold mine in southwest Wales.

Today, archaeologists are still unravelling the secrets of the various kilns and furnaces uncovered in the British Isles. Their clues include traces of ore and metal, signs of high-temperature effects on stonework around the hearth, and accumulated dross. Celtic mining and metalworking techniques may remain somewhat obscure, but there is ample evidence of their tremendous importance. ⊕ ⊕ ⊕

Gifts of the Sea

In lonely places along the coast, we can still hear the echo of Celtic songs sung by women as they collected seaweed and edible shellfish. Here they found both driftwood and amber, the yellow fossilised resin that was valuable for bead-making and used by the craftsmen to decorate their metalwork. What did these early people think of the driftwood lying among the wrack blown in by the winter storms? Bleached and smoothed by the waves, some pieces resembled sea monsters, others twisted sea-snakes, or the head of some ancient goddess. Driftwood was fashioned into handles for awls or toys for the children. Larger pieces were used to make furniture, or to supplement the hearth fire. Even today, mystery haunts these wonderful beaches, where rock pools shine like gleaming jewels and brightly coloured sea shells pattern the strand.

Seaweed of many kinds was gathered to make soups and stews. Kelp, for example, was the basis for a vegetable stew. Cut into strips, it was simmered briefly, then combined with root vegetables like parsnip to make a nourishing dish cooked slowly over a peat fire. Other uses of seaweed as food are described in chapter 4. ⊕ ⊕ ⊕

health and personal Appearance

Ammianus Marcellinus, who wrote in the sixth century, quoting from a much earlier text, reported that: "The Gauls [Celts] are all exceedingly careful of cleanliness and neatness; not in all the country...could any man or woman, however poor, be seen either dirty or ragged". The Celtic custom of bathing was legendary, and the practice of washing their hair before going into battle was characteristic. They washed each night before retiring, and every household had a tub for that purpose. "Feet-washing" was traditionally offered to guests on arrival.

Many of the tisanes and herbal infusions prepared today as "alternative" remedies or aromatherapy compounds have their origins in Celtic healing lore. Phoenician and Celtic traders had access to many herbs and spices, not only from the Mediterranean region, but from southern Arabia, India and even China. Indigenous plants used in healing included the seaweed carrageen, used in a hot drink including rosehip syrup as a cough remedy, and the herb ground ivy, prepared as a tisane for tonic use.

Special steam-houses were constructed by the Celts, small beehive-shaped enclosures built of stone and roofed with

OCCUPATIONS AND SKILLS

ling (heather) and turves. Pans of water, more often wooden troughs, were put inside the building and then brought to the boil by heating stones on a fire beside the building and rolling the hot stones down an incline into the troughs of water. Sufficient steam was generated to make an ideal sauna—a cure for rheumatism and chest complaints.

Beards and moustaches were favoured among the men. Historians tell us that short beards were worn, and some men let their moustaches grow so long that their mouths were covered. Many carvings and engravings of the Celtic period depict men with moustaches, and some Celtic bodies preserved in peat bogs show carefully trimmed beards and moustaches and manicured finger- and toenails. This concern with personal appearance is reflected in some of the grave goods, which include mirrors, manicure articles and other toilet items. ⊕ ⊕ ⊕

Soap and Perfume Making

A number of herb and flower infusions were prepared and used to perfume soap and other products. A simple infusion was made by pouring a quantity of water over the leaves or flowers of a herb, then leaving them to cool in a covered vessel. Some herb extracts were made by pouring melted tallow or oil over the herb, which was left to diffuse for several weeks in a warm place. The fat or oil absorbed the herb's essential oil.

Elderflower soap was considered softening, cleansing and soothing to the skin; dandelion root and leaves, tonic and cleansing; burdock root and leaves, astringent and invigorating. Lovage leaves were used as a deodorant, and the root extract was esteemed as cleansing and astringent.

Honey soap, perfumed with sweet marjoram, was made by taking 9 parts of soft soap to 1 part of honey and gently melting them together. The marjoram was added by way of a strong infusion of the herb in water, a little of the water being added to the soap. Then the warm liquid was allowed to solidify in moulds.

It is from some of the early Celtic recipes that we derive many toilet waters and lotions on the market today. Elderflower water similar to that made by the Celts can be

obtained by adding 3½ oz (100 g) of the petals to 14 fl oz (400 ml) of water. Let stand for ten minutes, then distil using a distilling flask and condenser. The distillate should be bottled and left to mature until it develops a pleasant aroma. It can be mixed with anhydrous lanolin or made into a lotion. Rosewater can be made in the same way. Add the rose petals (those of *Rosa damascena* are best) to water and distil as above.

Astringent lotions were made by infusing rosemary, elder-flowers and sage with honey vinegar (or wine vinegar) for two or three weeks; the infusion was then strained for use. Two tablespoons of the vinegar infusion were put into a basin of warm water and used to wash the skin or as a hair rinse after shampooing.

Lavender (*Lavendula angustifolia*), native to the Mediter-ranean region, was introduced into Britain by the Celts. This hardy and aromatic plant was valued not only for its distinctive, sweet perfume, but for the aromatic smoke pro-duced by burning the dried flower heads. When the flower spikes are distilled, the yield of oil is between 0.8 and 1 percent, and the essential oil produced in Britain is still the best in the world. If lavender is steeped in white wine vinegar, with a pinch of rosemary added, it can be an effec-

tive headache remedy when dabbed on the forehead and temples. It was believed that lavender oil could neutralise the venom of a viper.

A farrier's soap for the treatment of skin diseases in ponies was prepared from fish oil and seaweed extract, the latter providing iodine and other salts, the soap being prepared with seaweed-ash lye. Another additive to give a very fine polish to metal was rottenstone (a soft stone derived from the breakdown of silaceous limestone). This material was incorporated into a soap and made a polish, not only for metal, but to give a high lustre to horn and bone used to make spoons, drinking horns and decorative items. Another soap that was in great demand was for cleaning and scouring wool. This fuller's soap was prepared as a soft soap with soft water, lye and refined lard. ⊕ ⊕ ⊕

Celtic Craftsmanship

To decorate ornamental artefacts, the Celtic craftworker used many materials, including native minerals, coloured glass, and amber, the fossil resin that was credited with magical and medicinal properties. Minerals included garnet, which varies in colour from red and violet to yellowish-red, and rock crystal (pure silica), a colourless quartz. Large pieces were made into cups and vases; smaller pieces were used in jewellery.

In all kinds of ornamentation, the Celts used swirling curvilinear decoration. Their early designs included concentric circles, angular and geometric patterns and whorls. Later, they employed plain and animal interlace, La Tene scrolls, heads and animal faces, zoomorphic and unstylised in any ritual sense (except for later Christian artefacts). This development represented an explosion of abstract art, all-embracing, compelling and unique.

Artistically and technically, the Celtic artisan reached a peak just before the Roman invasion of Britain, although in the north and west, and in Ireland, where the Romans never set foot, the old tradition remained. It would reflourish in the Celtic Renaissance.

Bones, and bone fragments, bearing elaborate decorative designs have been discovered, as, for example, those found in a Celtic reoccupation of a megalithic passage-grave in Ireland. Initially, it was thought that these designs were trial pieces for decoration of bronze working, although no trace of metalworking has been found at the site. The motifs on these pieces are superb and can be seen at the National Museum of Ireland in Dublin. One particular design on the Lough Crew (County Meath) bone flakes is repeated in the design on a broken decorated stone from Derrykeighan. This strengthens the evidence that artists and travelling pattern-makers produced design-work for use by craftsmen (and scribes) elsewhere.

Celtic craftsmen—blacksmiths, braziers, wheelwrights and carpenters—combined their skills to produce two- and four-wheeled wagons, racing and war chariots, covered wagons for merchandise and weapons far in advance of those produced elsewhere. Other specialised craftsmen included saddlers, furniture makers, shoemakers, button makers, weavers and dyers and herbalists. There must also have been skilled practitioners of medicine and surgery, for archaeologists have found metal items that could have been designed only for surgical operations.

OCCUPATIONS AND SKILLS

As mentioned earlier, ancient methods of mining and refining gold, silver, tin, copper and iron were improved by Celtic foundrymen and metalworkers, who also developed new metal alloys for special purposes. Kaolin is china clay that has been thoroughly washed in many changes of water to remove all sand and other gritty substances. A fine-quality kaolin is found in Cornwall; it is particularly white and workable and was mined by the Celts. This clay is formed by the weathering of feldspar in granite rock, where repeated frosts and decomposition have broken it down to a fine dust-like material. Specially prepared varieties of kaolin were, and are still, used in place of fuller's earth as dusting and toilet powders.

These skills were instrumental in building a secure society, wherein warriors gave the craftsman and farmer the freedom to pursue their occupations. Thus the society progressed from one of hunter-gatherers, subject to the vagaries of nature and threats from aggressive neighbours, to one in which material resources could be developed for both sustenance and trade. ⊕ ⊕ ⊕

Everyday Dress and "High Fashion"

Workmen, Warriors and Noblewomen

In manner of dress and clothing, there was a recognised style among the Celts that indicated social status, but in general the dress of men, women and children was similar. The basic garment was a linen or woollen tunic, often worn with short or long breeches. Over these, a cloak or mantle was either wrapped around the body several times or draped loosely from the shoulder and caught at the neck with a brooch or fibula.

The torque (or torc), worn around the neck, was made of twisted metal and denoted the wearer's status in the community. It also had ritual significance, and torques were often hereditary, serving as symbols of authority over the family or tribe.

Wild and domestic animals provided fur and leather for outer garments and cloaks. Sheep-raising enabled manufacture of woollen clothing. The Celts developed a strain of sheep whose fleece could be plucked or combed: the animals were not sheared. Where flax was grown, linen was made, especially for undergarments.

The importation of material from distant countries enabled wealthy Celts to wear exotic fabrics, which they decorated

with their own characteristic flamboyance, and there was a trade in jewellery from the earliest days of Celtic society. From about 250 BC, Celtic noblemen and -women had access by trade to silk and other luxurious fabrics, as well as spices and jewels sent into southern Arabia from the Far East and exported overland to western Europe. Young women, up to marriageable age, customarily did not cover their upper bodies within the homestead, which led to a highly developed art of body-painting.

Fine leather was used for special garments, similar to chamois leather, but made from sheepskin. It had a soft, pliable texture well suited to the art of the needlewoman. Heavier clothing was made from skins and hides, used also for domestic floor and bed coverings. Leather belts were generally decorated with incised designs, laid in with colour or with metallic thread and studs. The art of tanning reached a high degree among the Celts, as described on pages 61 to 63.

Craftsmen wore leather aprons for heavy work, and the woodsman, farmer and hunter wore leather or cloth leggings to protect the lower leg from thorn bushes. These were similar in purpose to the chaps (from the Spanish *chaparajos*) worn by American cowboys on the range.

CELTIC DAILY LIFE

Some Celtic warriors (the *gaesatae*) went into battle quite naked, except for a baldric slung from the shoulder across the chest. By ancient custom, their bodies were decorated with elaborate symbols and designs using the blue dye called indigo, derived from the herb woad. Horsemen and charioteers wore breeches with straps crossing under the foot of each trouser leg to prevent their riding up the calf.

In matters of costume and beautification, the Celtic belle compared favourably with Greek and Roman ladies, and the men were equally well turned out. The demand for elaborately designed and embroidered clothing led naturally to high-quality home spinning and weaving. Fabrics were dyed with natural colours derived from mosses and a host of other local plants, including poppies, larkspur, red vetch and lichens. Thus certain groups of Celtic families or tribes wore similarly coloured garments, which eventually gave rise to the misnamed "clan tartan". ⊕ ⊕ ⊕

Working with Pelts and Hides

The Celts used the hides of animals killed for food for a variety of products, and large quantities of hides were available in the late autumn when cattle were killed to be preserved for winter food. The term "hide" (*seite*) refers to large, heavy skins, like those of cows, horses or oxen. Skins of such small mammals as hares, moles and squirrels are termed pelts. When freshly taken from the animal, the skin was known as the "green skin"; after salt-curing it was referred to as the "salt skin".

The Celtic tanner knew that as soon as a skin was removed from the carcase, there was every danger that it would deteriorate unless treated promptly. Dry salting was the first stage in preservation. This was done by putting the skin onto a flat board and rubbing salt—approximately half the weight of the skin—into the flesh side by hand. The edges of the skin were turned up so that the salt was contained. Pure, fine-grain salt was used, as rough-grain salt, such as untreated sea salt, is unsuitable. Larger sheepskins were fashioned into rugs or wall coverings, while smaller ones were used to make clothing and other items for domestic use.

The Celts used a process similar to oil tanning to make leather ropes and harness reins. Generally speaking, the hide of an ox was used for this purpose. The hide was steeped in water to loosen the hair, which was then pulled out painstakingly by hand. After the hide was scraped completely clean, it was cut into strips, from 1 inch (2.5 cm) to 3 inches (7.5 cm) wide. If very long ropes or reins were needed, the hide was cut in a circular-spiral mode so that one hide produced a single length. These strips were then hung from a tree branch with a heavy weight (such as a stone) tied to the lower end to keep the hide taut. The strips were then oiled with a mixture of fish oil and lard and twisted for approximately a week, after which the leather rope or harness strips were ready for use.

The use of vegetable extracts like tannin to preserve and colour hides came later. Tannin is obtained from the bark of several trees, notably the oak. Its bark contains from 15 to 17 percent of tannin, and oak tannin produces a very bright leather. Oak-galls (or nut-galls), which are formed on the tree as a result of wasp damage, contain up to 60 percent of tannin, and their extract was also used to make writing ink. Tannin made from the wood of the chestnut tree gives leather a dark, reddish-brown colour.

Everyday Dress and "High Fashion"

To obtain tannin from the oak, the bark was first stripped away with a specially shaped flint or bronze tool. The stripping had to be done carefully, or the tree would be killed. The bark was then either stored in a dry shed until needed, or broken up immediately by cutting and crushing. The tannin was then extracted by a process called leaching, which consisted of heating the crushed bark with soft water repeatedly. The Celts used a series of wooden troughs in which they placed the crushed bark. The first trough was filled with boiling soft water and allowed to stand. The water was then drained off and the extract boiled and added to the second trough of crushed bark. The process was repeated until a strong tanning solution was achieved. Powdered tannin is a complex chemical entity, brownish to light yellow in colour. Tannin solutions react with iron salts to produce an inky-black colour: thus all traces of iron must be excluded for all uses except the preparation of ink. The Celts developed a sophisticated knowledge of the preparation of tannin and other vegetable extracts for use in working with hides for clothing. ⊕ ⊕ ⊕

Oʒeınʒ and Weavınʒ

The linen or woollen *tunica*, described by the historian Strabo, was made with a very fine weave, using dyed yarn; occasionally, the garment was dyed after being made up, and then embroidered. These tunics were worn ankle-length by women and knee-length or slightly longer by men. They were drawn in at the waist with a belt or girdle of metal links, leather or woven material.

Before a piece of fleece or wool can be dyed, it must first be scoured to remove any excess grease or oil from the material. The Celts probably treated the fibres with an alkaline mixture. They began the scouring process by combining the alkaline with a concentrated extract, known as lye or pearl-ash, from pieces of wood or ashes of kelp. The wool was first soaked and gently agitated, after which it was removed and placed into a mixture of hot, soapy water to remove excess alkali. Once the wool was completely rinsed, it was then drained and laid to dry in the shade.

The next stage of the dyeing proccess was to create a mordant solution. The most common mordants (metallic compounds used to fix the colour) used by the Celts were alum, chrome, iron and tin, all of which are highly harmful when

concentrated. Each of these substances produces a different result: alum yields clear and well-defined tones; chrome gives deep and mellow shades; iron compounds produce dull shades; and tin will result in bright and vibrant colours.

The mordant was dissolved in a basin of hot water. When the temperature of the solution was tepid, the scoured wool was slightly dampened and submerged in the basin. The basin was then placed over a fire until the solution reached the boiling point. After allowing the wool to simmer, it was removed and plunged into the simmering dye bath for fixing.

Any number of herbs, plants, roots and bark were used to make dyes. Agrimony, which is still found growing freely in Britain, gives a fawn colour with chrome mordant, and the whole plant can be used—flowers, stems and leaves. Dandelion roots and leaves give a deep shade of fawn with alum; onion skins combined with a tin mordant yield deep orange; and horsetail and alum produce light yellow shades.

Yellow was also prepared from weld, or wild mignonette (*Reseda luteola*), an ancient dye plant widely cultivated in Britain for this purpose. In addition to providing a yellow dye, its juice is used to make an artist's colour called Dutch Pink. Weld is a biennial plant and grows almost everywhere, although it prefers a fairly dry, non-acidic soil. It reaches

a height of six feet (2 metres) and can be cultivated in most gardens. The flowers are more green than yellow, and the leaves are undivided and usually deeply lobed. An extract from the plant was also used as a sedative. Weld gives a very bright yellow with an alum mordant and a blend of shades can be used if other dyes are combined. For example, when used with blue it will give a magnificent green.

Red shades can be made using madder (*Rubia tinctorum*), which is easily grown in the garden. The flowers are single at the top of the branches, and the fruit is a berry, red at first, turning to black and containing two yellow seeds. The dye is obtained from the root of the plant. Once cultivated extensively, it can now be found growing wild in many areas in southern Britain. Combined with an alum mordant, madder dye will yield a rose-red shade. Chrome mordant produces reddish-brown shades.

The fine weaving achieved by the Celts resulted from their skill in interlacing the two sets of yarns—warp and weft, or filling—on the loom. The yarn count and number of warp and filling yarns to the quare inch determined the closeness or looseness of a weave.

Until the end of the seventeenth century, the craft of weaving linen from flax was the principal cottage indus-

try in Scotland; the use of linen clothing was derived from the early Celts in Ireland. To encourage linen manufacture, an act was passed in Scotland in 1686 mandating burial in "Scots linen", but after the Union (1707), it was rescinded by the decree that "no corpse shall be buried in linen…plain woollen cloth…shall only be made use of". At that time, the woollen industry was essential to the English economy, and the new ruling provided industrialists with an additional market. However, an even more important objective of the new law was the erosion of age-old Celtic custom. This would not be the last of a series of proscriptions aimed at destroying Celtic tradition in Scotland. ⊕ ⊕ ⊕

Cloaks into Kilts

The men's cloak or mantle was worn in a variety of styles and colours. The Irish cloak had no hood or sleeves, and its length denoted the social status of the wearer—five-folded for kings and chiefs, three-folded for warriors. Many cloaks were adorned with colourful braid or fringes. These garments gave rise to the present-day kilt, which is known as the plaid, from the Gaelic *plaide*, a blanket.

Over the centuries, the cloak evolved into some seventeen feet of double-width cloth, pleated and buckled about the waist and often worn with hose of contrasting check. Although Englishman John Taylor, in 1618, mentioned the "stuffe of diverse colours which they call Tartane", the idea that specific tartans related to specific families or clans during this and earlier eras is incorrect. Tartans—coloured patterning—were produced entirely to the cottagers' own design, and their colours depended on vegetable dyes available locally. Clan or family connections were for many centuries purely incidental. After visiting the Western Isles in 1703, MacLeod wrote: "Every isle differs from each other in their fancy of making plaids, as to the stripes and breadth of colours....These patterns and colours...are [just] as different through the main-

land of the Highlands, in-so-far that they who have seen those places are able, at the first view of a man's plaid, to guess the place of his residence". Thus we can be sure that by the early 1700s, certain patterns and colours were associated with different geographical areas, but the idea that clans had their own exclusive tartans was not conceived until a century after the battle of Culloden (1746).

To dress in the plaid, the belt was laid on the ground and the material folded lengthwise into pleats and placed on top of the belt. The wearer then stretched himself out upon the plaid, folding the material over the front of the body and fastening the belt around the waist. The result was a pleated kilt with a mass of material above the waist, which was either brought over the left shoulder or drawn around shoulders and chest for warmth. The modern kilt is simply the lower half of the belted plaid with the pleats stitched.

The *skean dhu* (black knife) that still forms a part of traditional Celtic dress is derived from the short dirk or dagger that was invariably carried by men both for hunting purposes and as a table knife. Now worn at the right calf as a part of the traditional kilted Celtic outfit, it was formerly carried attached to the sword, except in combat, when it was attached to the belt by a chain or leather strap. ⊕ ⊕ ⊕

haiRsτɣℓes and Cosmeτics

The Celts considered beautiful hair the most important adornment. It was often referred to in legends of the Land of the Ever Young, as in the story of Etain, who was described as having "two plaits of golden hue upon her head, each plait woven out of four tresses, and a ball of gold upon the end of every tress".

Women often coloured and streaked their hair to complement their costumes. Whole locks of hair were gathered up and coloured in different shades, so that when it was plaited, by interlacing three or more strands, the alternating colours gave a pleasing and decorative appearance. Often, the plaits were woven so that two circled the brow and others hung at either side of the head and down the back, sometimes interlaced with gold or silver thread. Waist-length hair was commonplace. According to the Roman historian Dion Cassius, Boudicca, the warrior queen of the Iceni, had a mass of bright red hair that fell to her knees.

The warrior wore his hair long and full, at least to shoulder length, and it was customary to wash the hair and to bathe before joining battle. On ceremonial occasions, warriors whitened their hair with lime and water; sometimes

they drew it out into long spikes with a carefully prepared mixture of beeswax, oil and honey.

Hair rinses were prepared by making an infusion of birch twigs in soft water, which conditioned and gave lustre to the hair, and extracts of herbs and spices were compounded from vinegar, which was diluted with soft water before use and perfumed with petals. Pomades combined beeswax, perfume and refined wool fat or lanolin.

Perfumes, obtained from flower petals or herbs, were readily available, and scented material was chewed to sweeten the breath. In many a ballad, we learn that the heroine had "breath sweet smelling of thyme and honey, as lovely as the perfumed summer breeze". Body lotions were applied after bathing, and the bath water itself was perfumed with herbs and petals. Eye shadows in complementary shades were used, and talcum powder, perfumed and tinted, was applied to the arms and shoulders. Lips were tinted in various colours, often to match hair colouring and garments.

Lanolin, or wool-fat, was preferable to lard for making lotions and cosmetic creams, as it is closely allied to the skin's natural secretion. Lanolin was obtained by kneading combed sheeps' wool in water to obtain an emulsion that the housewife and wisewoman processed for cosmetic use.

Facial cleansing and rejuvenating creams were prepared by combining herbal infusions of various kinds with melted beeswax, lanolin and small quantities of kaolin. Prepared over a water-bath, these creams were then cooled and stored in cosmetic jars. Purified lard was combined with fragrant herbs and strained through a fine cloth to make a base for pomades. To make a modern-day version of the Celtic cleansing facial treatment, melt four teaspoons of beeswax in a small dish on a water-bath, then add four teaspoons of anhydrous lanolin. Stir over the water-bath until blended. Slowly add 9 fl oz (250 ml) of a strong herbal infusion, which has been prepared by steeping 2 oz (55 g) of the dried herb in a pint (550 ml) of boiling soft water. Leave to stand for 24 hours, then warm the infusion and add it slowly to the melted beeswax and lanolin. Stir until thoroughly mixed, then add some three tablespoons of kaolin a little at a time, stirring into a paste. When cool, store in small jars. ⊕ ⊕ ⊕

Adornments and Jewellery

The Celts were highly skilled in metalwork, and popular appreciation of Celtic artistry, design and craftsmanship has only increased with the passage of time. The principal raw material used for their personal adornments was iron. Certain iron minerals were used to make jewellery. Haematite, for example, served as a charm. The polished ore was pierced and worn as necklace, interspersed with pierced gold, crystals or amber, for its clear and beautiful contrast.

Gold, a soft, durable and non-corrosive metal, was used to make jewellery, as well as to embellish sword-hilts and scabbards and to apply decoration to the surface of drinking vessels and ornaments. Because of the relative scarcity of gold, other metals were sometimes gilded with beaten gold, in which case the base metal, say, iron, was highly polished, then heated. The gold leaf was applied and gently pressed down with a burnisher, then re-exposed to heat. Additional layers were applied in the same fashion, and the last layer burnished when it was cold. Burnishers were made of a dog's tooth, or a hard material like agate, fixed into a wooden handle. The burnisher itself was finely polished before it was used.

Celtic Daily Life

Bracelets were made of various metals in many styles. The Gaulcross hoard (discovered at Fordyce in Banffshire) includes a silver bracelet that takes the form of a spiral, a style adopted by both Celts and Picts. At Lydney (in Gloucestershire) and other temple sites in southern Britain, many bracelets have been found, perhaps used as votive offerings made at a shrine. These offerings may be connected with a marital occasion, the birth of a baby, the death of a loved one, or recovery from sickness. Armlets were also made from a variety of metals, some of considerable weight, others lighter and embellished with gilt and enamel and decorated with elaborate designs and filigree (ornamental metallic lacework).

Filigree was characteristic of Celtic workmanship and much in demand. The filigree material comprised wires and metallic particles or globules, often soldered onto gold foil, which formed the backplate. This backplate was fixed to the metal either by rivets, clasps cut from the metal surface, or lap-joints. Since gold and silver are ductile and easily worked, wire was originally made by preparing thin, square section rods, which were then twisted and finally rolled between two flat plates. This plain wire could be made into beaded wire by tapping the material along its length in a patterned die, or between two patterned dies,

to produce special effects. Simple strands of wire were often twisted together to form a plaited effect, and sometimes a beaded wire was twined with two plain wires to produce a rich embellishment.

Celtic jewellery was often decorated by inlay of North Sea amber, coral, precious and semiprecious stones and glass. Niello (black inlay of various metal alloys) and enamelling were also used extensively in design work. Glass inlay was accomplished by heating the glass until it softened, then pressing it into place with recessed tools. Amber was similarly treated after softening with heat.

A great deal of decorative metal jewellery was cast, and many moulds have been found on Celtic sites. Castings were usually done in two pieces. Prepared clay was rolled into two balls, and one side of each was pressed flat against a board. The pattern of the piece to be cast—perhaps a brooch or decorative stud—was made in wax or lead, then pressed into the flat surface of one of the pieces of clay. This was then cut with a knife to give a pouring funnel and the resulting mould keyed and left to dry. The surface was then coated thinly with animal fat, and the flat surface of the second piece of clay was pressed against the first. This picked up the "negative" of the impression on the first piece. The two sections of the mould were then separated and the

pattern carefully refined. The mould was then joined together and fired; finally, the molten metal was poured in. When cold, the casting was removed and finished by "fettling", that is, filing, scraping and polishing.

Finger and thumb rings were made of various materials, including polished amber, tin and enamelled copper, or precious metals, and some were inlaid with mosaic settings. Some rings were cast in one piece, while others were of spiral form. They sometimes served as tokens of recognition, as did the signet ring of later ages, and could be given to another person to carry as a sign of delegation of authority by the owner to the bearer, his messenger.

At Whitby, Yorkshire, jet (fossilised wood from the sea, swamps and riverbeds) was fashioned into necklaces, bracelets, brooches and rings. Stone Age people used it to make decorative amulets, and Neolithic men also formed it into jewellery. They broke the jet into suitably sized pieces, then shaped and polished it after mixing its dust and oil into a paste. This was placed on a flat stone and the piece of jet rubbed against it until smooth and polished. The Celts began mining jet at Whitby, still the world's best source for hard jet. Workshops there produced magnificent pieces that were exported to Gaul.

Everyday Dress and "High Fashion"

Enamelled and engraved brooches were of remarkable design and workmanship, like those of the Ardagh hoard and the pieces found at Ballynaglogh, Hunterston, Blair Atholl and Dunkeld. Pins and plaques, dress-fasteners and buckles, were all elaborately decorated and often enamelled in rich colours. Most Celts carried a small ornamental bag, those of the women containing such items as comb, eyebrow dye and lip salve or rouge. The sporran of the Highland Gael, worn about the waist, is derived from this Celtic and Pictish custom. ⊕ ⊕ ⊕

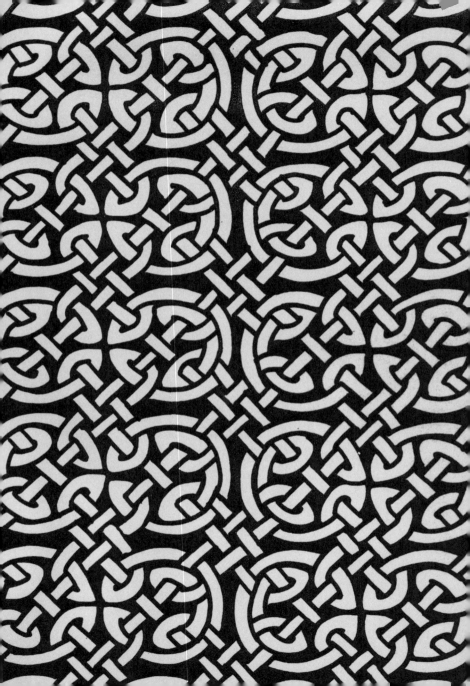

Food, Drink
and
Herb Lore

Foods Grown, Gathered and Stored

The ability of the Celts to grow and, in fact, to develop new strains of grain, and their skill as herdsmen, fishermen and hunters, provided them with a wide range of foodstuffs. We have learned much about their domestic life from the blackened ashes of their cooking hearths and the artefacts found in graves and ruined hill-forts. And there is still a traditional way of cooking among Celtic families, who have passed down their recipes through generations.

Grain was stored to supply seed for the next sowing and to meet the annual demand for domestic use and for use as an ingredient in beer-making. It was kept either in pits, particularly on well-drained chalk soil, or above ground in storage bins. The storage pit was made by digging a hole with the proper ratio of diameter to depth, which was critical. The pit was lined with wicker and flint, the grain put in and the top covered by a capstone sealed with clay. Natural moisture allowed some of the grain to germinate. During germination, the sprouting seed produces carbon dioxide, an inert gas in which moulds and microbes cannot grow. Thus the carbon dioxide acted as a preservative to keep the grain in good condition.

Above-ground storage bins (or silos) were built either on well-drained ground or on wooden or stone stilts; guard dogs kept vermin and other pests away. Since a low moisture content is essential for grain storage, double-skin structures were often used. The exterior cladding kept rain and snow out, and an interior framework of tough, supple twigs like willow allowed air to circulate between outer and inner walls, preventing condensation.

A variety of animal fats and fish oils were available to the Celts, and those living in coastal areas had access to seal oil. Seed and nut oil was obtained by removing the shells and seed coat, then crushing and grinding. The oil was then "warmed out" by immersion in hot water and skimmed from the surface.

The leafy plant known as Fat-hen (*Chenopodium album*), which grows almost anywhere, figured largely in Celtic diet. The seeds contain fat and albumen and have been eaten or baked into bread since Neolithic times. The leaves have a higher food value than cabbage or spinach. Fat-hen grows from 1 to 3 feet (up to a metre) high, and the leaves vary from narrow to broad lanceolate. The small flowers are green or mealy-white. The plant was being cultivated as early as 300 BC. In fact, it was used as a vegetable until

well into the eighteenth century in Scotland and Ireland; in the Western Isles, it was called wild pottage. The leaves were boiled, pounded with butter and generally eaten with bacon and other meats. In recent times, it has been replaced by spinach. The Anglo-Saxons knew the plant as Melde: in Ireland, it is called Milds or Miles. (The name Melde gave rise to the place name Milden in Suffolk.)

Celtic families living near the sea used seaweed to supplement their diets and to make gels for thickening soups. Bladderwrack, carrageen, tangle, dulse and laver were harvested. Dulse is a red seaweed with a unique, spicy flavour, still in use today. It is plentiful on the Atlantic seacoast. Purple-red in colour, it has smooth, flat fronds from 6 to 18 inches (15–40 cm) long. Collected at low tide from May to November, the fronds were dried in the sun, then stored in airtight containers. They were used by the Celtic cook and wise woman for a number of recipes, including oatmeal and dulse soup.

Seaweed contains several valuable food elements, including sodium, potassium, iodine and magnesium. Kelp, also known as tangle or wrack, is a brown seaweed showing considerable variation in form. It has bright, glistening fronds and is prevalent along the Atlantic seaboard and

washed up among rocks and shingle. Casseroles of kelp and barley were prepared by soaking several fronds of kelp in fresh water overnight with washed barley, then boiling together for a short time.

Laver, as it is commonly known in Wales, or slake (Gaelic) and sloke (Irish), is *Porphyra laciniata*, an edible seaweed that grows at medium depths. There are several varieties, still used as foodstuffs. The bright-green form is often seen as a garnish, and the purple-frond variety in soups and salads. The laver called sea-lettuce is simply boiled and used as a vegetable.

Another highly prized delicacy long harvested on the coasts is not a seaweed but a herb, samphire, which grows on cliffs and along the base of beach rocks. Rock samphire (*Crithmum maritimum*) was once abundant, but is now common only in Cornwall and on the south coast of England. There were quantities on the Yorkshire coast, on Carnelian Bay near Scarborough and on the sandy beaches of the Lincolnshire coast (Saltfleetby, for example). Samphire was used as a vegetable and was frequently pickled.

The abundant foods grown and gathered by the early Celts were cooked over fires of wood, peat or heather. The destruction of the ancient British forests had begun as early

as Neolithic times, when people burned sections of the woodland to clear pasture for their animals and ground for cultivation. As the people moved on, more areas were burnt, and the loss of forest trees continued through Celtic, Viking, Saxon and Norman times. Wood was needed not only for cooking but for domestic fires, ship-building and the construction of houses; iron refining required wood or charcoal. In many areas, the stripped land grew mosses and peats that replaced the diminishing wood supply on the family hearth.

Although a peat fire may look dull by comparison with a wood fire, the aroma of burning peat is always delightful. The dark, heavy peats give the greatest heat and are the slowest burning; lighter coloured peats, which contain a larger percentage of roots, stalks and only partially reduced ling, give a brighter blaze but are not long-burning. In the cottage, the peats are kept beside the hearth, and their precise lay depends on when they are likely to be used on the fire. A peat fire can be smothered-in with thick, dry peats laid on top and covered over with wetter peats which are closely laid. Such a fire will last for three days or more. ⊕ ⊕ ⊕

Grain and Cereal Foods

A major breakthrough in Celtic agricultural techniques was the cultivation of the oat (Celtic, *coirce*) from a genus of wild grass plants (*Avena*) common to Europe and Britain. Some species became valuable for the grain they produced, which the Celts first used as a food for ponies. Later, oats were bred selectively to become a staple food. Oats were used in two ways: groats, which are oats from which the husks have been entirely removed by grinding and winnowing, and oatmeal, which is the meal inclusive of the husk.

Oats and other grains were prepared for cooking by cleaning and then grinding to different degrees of fineness in a quern. The first grinding was done with a wider gap between the stones, which enabled the hulls to be removed. A second grinding was much finer and produced the wholemeal flour from which bread, cakes and other foods were made. After the rotary quern came into use, the grains were fed into it through a hopper-like opening at the top. The upper stone was then rotated by a wooden handle fixed into a specially cut socket at one side. The stone rotated around a sturdy pivot made of wood or iron.

From hand-operated mills, larger stone mills were developed, rotated by oxen pulling against an arm fitted to a central drive. Later, the Celts developed a horizontal water mill that evolved into the vertical mill wheel of a later time, driven by water power controlled by gates or sluices.

Flour made from barley, oats and spelt (wheat) was used in many different ways, from porridge to sweet cakes. For a long time, wheat was little used in the northern counties of England and Scotland; oatmeal has been the staple of Irish and Scottish cuisine for centuries. The method of making simple porridge was to take a handful of oatmeal for each person, a cupful of water and a saltspoon of salt. When the water boiled, the oatmeal was dropped into it slowly while stirring. When the porridge boiled, the pot was covered and the mixture cooked gently for perhaps ten minutes. Then the salt was added, and cooking continued for another fifteen minutes or so.

Brose and stirabout were once the almost universal breakfast. Brose was made by pouring boiling milk, or the liquor in which meat had been boiled, onto oatmeal or barleymeal and stirring vigorously. Sometimes butter was added, and a sprinkling of ground caraway. Stirabout is an ancient dish made by pouring drippings over oatmeal or barleymeal. This

mixture was cooked in a frying pan with constant stirring. The word brose is derived from the Celtic *brothas* and has the same root as brew and broth. Stirabout is Anglo-Saxon, from *stiren*, to stir; the original Celtic word has been lost.

Barley and other breads were baked in an iron oven (or "baker") that was made in two parts: a heavy, flat base and a large domed cover with a sturdy handle on top. The base was set on a three-legged iron tripod, and a fire of bramble and wood was kindled beneath it. The cover was put in place, and when red hot, the wood was cleared from around the baker (top part), which was then lifted, and the dough, in iron pots (like baking tins), was placed on the base and re-covered. Then burning wood and kindling were placed around and over it. Excellent bread and cakes could be made in these ovens in about half an hour.

An alternative to baking in the oven was to use a single flat iron plate, now known as a girdle (or griddle), with a handle fitted to one side. This was heated over a fire and used in preparing, for example, the pancakes known in the Orkney Islands as Tea Pancakes. Traditional Orkney pancakes can be prepared from the following ingredients: 1 teacupful wholemeal flour; 1 saltspoon salt; 1 egg; 1 tablespoon honey (or fine sugar); and enough milk to make a

creamy batter. Beat up the egg, sift the flour into a bowl and mix in the salt and sugar. Slowly add enough milk, while mixing, to make a batter about the consistency of thin cream, stirring continuously. Add the egg and beat well. Have a fairly hot girdle ready, and grease it by rubbing it with a piece of suet wrapped in a clean cloth. Put a large tablespoon of batter on the girdle, spreading it thinly and evenly to make the pancake. It should brown very quickly; then turn it and brown the other side. (These Orkney Pancakes can also be made in a small omelette pan greased with lard.) Serve hot and spread with butter and honey (or jam).

Yeast is required for bread-making, and up to the early 1800s it was common practice to use yeast from beer brewing. The Celtic kitchen produced both beer and mead on an almost daily basis, and this supplied the yeast for the next brewing and also for bread-making. The thick deposit left in the beer vat after fermenting was allowed to settle. Then the liquid floating on the surface was removed and mixed with ten to twelve times the amount of fresh soft water. After stirring, the yeast was allowed to settle to the bottom. The surface liquid was poured off again and the deposit of yeast washed with additional water and allowed to resettle. The final deposit was used to make bread.

Baps, or Scottish Rolls, were a form of oval flatbread made from whole-grain flour, honey, lard, salt, yeast and a mixture of milk and water. Other popular breadstuffs included oatcake, pancakes and Irish soda bread.

Honey cake was a popular delicacy that we can replicate today with the following ingredients: 4 oz (110 g) wholemeal flour; an equal amount of butter; two eggs, well beaten; 1/2 oz (28 g) baker's yeast; and one cupful of warmed honey. Cream together the flour and butter, then add the warmed honey. Add the eggs gradually, mix thoroughly and let stand. Mix separately 1/2 oz baker's yeast, three tablespoons of tepid water and a teaspoon of honey. Then stand in a warm place for 10–15 minutes, until it has a head of foam. Add this to the dough mixture, beat well and leave in a warm place, covered with a damp cloth. When the dough has risen, knead well on a floured board. Place in a well-greased baking pan. Cover with a damp cloth and allow to rise in a warm place. Then bake in a hot oven. The top of the cooked honey cake may be covered with finely chopped hazel nuts mixed with honey to make a paste. ⊕ ⊕ ⊕

Meat and Fish

S elective breeding of cattle, sheep and pigs was a major breakthrough in Celtic agriculture. It became possible, too, where hay and roots were available as fodder, to maintain a large number of animals throughout the winter; thus they could be slaughtered when needed. Before that time, it had been customary to slaughter many animals in early winter: the flesh was preserved either by smoking, or with brine and vinegar. Advances in animal husbandry not only gave the Celt an economic edge over other tribes, but provided a better, more balanced diet that would directly result in a healthier population.

Pork was a delicacy that appeared frequently at the Celtic table, and vinegar was used to tenderise and break down the fibrous structure of the meat. These spice and herb vinegars became known later as marinades. A simple marinade for pork consisted of about 1 1/2 teaspoons each of thyme and cumin seeds, 3 cardamom pods, 3 teaspoons of salt and a little wild ramson (garlic) to taste. The mixture was pounded in a mortar, then placed in a basin and about half a pint of wine or honey vinegar added. After marinading overnight, the remaining liquor could be strained

to make a sauce, or used with oil added to it to baste the roast. Suckling pig stuffed with bread, sage, nutmeats and butter was a popular dish.

The traditional way to roast lamb was before a hot fire, either on a spit or hung from a fire-hook with the basting tray beneath to catch the drippings. The meat was far enough from the fire to prevent the fat from burning and was basted frequently.

Elderberry wine was used as a marinade base for lamb or venison. To half a pint of elderberry wine, wild ramson and a few bruised rosemary and melilot (aromatic clover) leaves were added. The marinade was simmered briefly before use. During the winter months, when people ate dried (smoked) or salted fish and meat, spiced vinegar and wine were used as marinades to improve flavour. Melilot, thyme, wild ramson and rosemary were staples that formed the basis of several wine and vinegar infusions.

Seafood was another staple item. According to the historian Atheaneus, "Those [Celts] who live beside the rivers or the Mediterranean or Atlantic eat [baked] fish,…with the addition of salt, vinegar and cummin". Seafoods available to Celts of the British Isles included salmon, trout, eel, pilchards, mackerel, herring, mussels and whitefish. The

fish were baked, grilled, smoked or sautéed and prepared with a variety of marinades and spices. Fish stews and steamed shellfish were nourishing components of the Celtic diet. A simple fish soup was made by melting butter, adding a small amount of flour and simmering with fish stock to which milk and parsley had been added. The seaweed dulse was often cooked with fish dishes and used as a garnish.

Salted eels and salmon were smoked for about three days over a choked fire of birch and oak leaves, juniper twigs and their berries. Some fish were "potted" for the table by methods that are still in use today. To make traditionally potted trout, fry the fish, and while it is still warm, lift the flesh in pieces from the bones and layer lengthwise in a buttered pie-dish. Sprinkle each layer with salt and pepper, then run melted butter over the whole. This dish is usually eaten cold. Pilchards, a rare delicacy, were marinaded and served cold as well; they were often prepared with spiced vinegar.

According to one recipe, fresh trout was prepared by salting the trout and leaving it overnight. In the morning, after wiping, the fish was dipped in milk and thickly coated with coarse oatmeal. Placed in a pan of smoking-hot lard, it was cooked for a few minutes until brown on both sides. After draining, it was often served with butter and a dash of

spiced vinegar. Mackerel were sometimes roasted with fennel, then opened and boned. A sauce of parsley and butter was popular, served hot with fish.

Almonds—blanched, peeled and split and sometimes combined with cummin—were a frequent accompaniment to barbecued fish. Almonds were also used in stuffing for game birds and chicken, made with cummin, fennel, honey, butter, ramsons and breadcrumbs. Barbecued fish and meat were commonly served on broad, sword-shaped skewers. ⊕ ⊕ ⊕

Beverages Including Mead and Wine

The drink of the wealthy classes was wine, which was imported from Italy or from Gaul. The lower classes drank wheaten beer prepared with a little honey. The question as to whether the Celts produced alcohol by distillation is still debated. Some antiquarians and archaeologists deny it; others, including this writer, believe that such processes were carried out.

The Celts were famous for the fermented honey beverage known to us as mead, an alcoholic drink that was consumed in Britain up to the end of the eighteenth century. It was used

regularly in the home and featured on all kinds of festive occasions. Indeed, the word "honeymoon" (originally honey-month) derives from the custom of drinking mead and feasting for twenty-eight days after a wedding. The Celtic host passed the mead bowl to guests at the table. The drink was also consumed at many religious festivals and ceremonial occasions. The basic recipe called for one part honey to three parts water, to which flavouring herbs and spices were added. Occasionally, a portion of dark ground malt was included. The mixture was then fermented.

Mead was also used in a variety of other ways. The Celts in Britain discovered that mead, left open and exposed to the air, soon turned sour, enabling them to produce honey vinegar; eventually, this developed into a small rural industry. Vinegar was important not only to the housewife, but to the rural craftsman. Artisans and fabric dyers used it in several of their processes. Pickling meats, fruits, vegetables and other foodstuffs in vinegar, with some salt added, preserved them. Both honey and wine vinegar gave piquancy and zest to many dishes, and in the absence of refrigeration, enabled the Celtic cook to develop new and improved recipes. Eventually, vinegars would be flavoured with such herbs as thyme, wild garlic and rosemary.

Food, Drink and Herb Lore

The Celtic housewife was well acquainted with fermentation processes. It was known that during the fermentation of beer, or of grape juice, bubbles came to the surface of the liquid so that it appeared to be boiling. (Of course, the fact that this bubbling was caused by carbon dioxide, liberated when the yeast cells converted the sugars into alcohol, was quite unknown.) Alcoholic liquids exposed to air for some time soon developed a leathery surface growth, and the liquid became acidic due to vinegar formation by bacterial action. The winemaker knew that air must be excluded from his product, which was done simply by pouring the wine into a narrow-necked container (an amphora, for example), then allowing boiled oil or fat to run into the neck of the vessel so that air could not enter.

The process of distillation was used, at least by the later Celts, to prepare concentrates used in making beverages and various household products. Early distillation flasks were shaped like the pottery feeder-flask, samples of which date back to the first millennium BC—they resemble a metal tea or coffee pot, but with the spout placed higher up the body. The liquid to be distilled was placed in the pot, the lid sealed on with lute (a special clay) and the contents boiled. The steam then streamed from the spout. This was

condensed and the distillate allowed to drip into a small receiver which stood in a bowl of cold water. When fresh water was not easily accessible, sea water could be desalinated for drinking purposes by this method.

The well-known Irish distilled spirit poteen (potheen) can be made from several starch-containing materials (potatoes are more often used today) as in Celtic times. According to this long-held tradition, the tubers should be lifted when their starch content is at a maximum and boiled under pressure so that the cell walls are broken down and the starch grains ruptured. The boiled potatoes are placed in a mash tun, and a little water is added together with some germinated barley (green malt). Then more water is added and the mash is boiled, next fermented and finally distilled to obtain alcohol. It is believed in Ireland that an infallible way to test the quality of poteen is to add a measure to a glass of milk. If the milk curdles, the poteen is of doubtful quality. The word poteen is a diminutive of the Gaelic *poit*. Good-quality poteen matured in casks is a very acceptable beverage and has retained its popularity through the centuries.

A non-alcoholic drink taken to the fields at harvest time to refresh the reapers was similar to the barley-water that is sold today. The drink is still made by pouring boiling

Food, Drink and Herb Lore

white wine vinegar over a handful of lemon-balm leaves and fresh heads. This is left to cool and infuse until the next day. In a separate basin, put three teaspoons of ground oatmeal, one teaspoon of honey and three teaspoons of the balm vinegar. Mix, then pour into the bowl 4 fl oz (110 ml) of boiling water. Stir and leave for ten to twenty minutes. Cool, and the drink is ready. At the end of the day, it was customary to mix this beverage with an equal amount of Celtic beer before supper. ⊕ ⊕ ⊕

household herbs and Flavourings

Celtic homesteads had rushes strewn on the floor for cleanliness and freshness, renewed by sweet herbs. Sweet flag, with its delightful aroma, was much prized, mixed with meadowsweet and woodruff. Infusions of aromatic herbs were made in water and sprinkled on the rushes. A curious, but obviously efficient sprinkler, found at Swallowcliffe Down, Wiltshire, was used for this purpose. Made of copper, it is in three parts. The hemisphere was soldered and the lower half pierced with small holes. The sprinkler was filled by immersing it in a bowl of perfumed liquid, and the flow of liquid through the holes was controlled by applying the thumb to the open end of the hollow handle. An ingenious Celtic innovation and an application of fundamental hydronamics!

Many herbs and edible flowers were used to flavour food and beverages, and such flavourings were sometimes quite elaborate. The taste of mead and beer was enhanced with various combinations of sweet briar petals, violet flowers, sweet marjoram, agrimony, bugloss, fennel and caraway. These were put into a bag, about a spoonful of each, and boiled along with the brew.

Horseradish, prepared with vinegar, was a popular flavouring of ancient origin. The plant can still be found growing wild in most parts of the British Isles. It is a deep-rooted perennial that will spread quickly when grown in the garden. The Celts used an infusion of horseradish in vinegar, or in milk, as a tonic.

Originally from China, Tibet and Northern India, rhubarb came to the British Isles many centuries ago by way of traders. It has deep green leaves on thick fleshy stalks, which are generally cooked and eaten as a fruit. Originally, the rhizome had a place in herbal medicine as a laxative and purgative. Today only the fleshy stem is eaten.

Dried saffron, from the autumn crocus, has a distinctive odour and bitterish taste. The Celts cultivated the bulb, and there was once a thriving industry in Britain, which gave us the place name of Saffron Walden. Some areas still show evidence of ancient cultivation, and the flower also grows wild, notably in Cornwall, one of the last Celtic strongholds, and in the Yorkshire Briganti country, where limestone pasture favours its growth. The Celts grew the plant in land that was not too wet. The planting was done in early summer, and in early autumn the blue flowers appeared. The saffron blades (that is, the stigmas) were dried inside small

beehive-shaped kilns made of clay and straw. The blades were spread thinly on shelves inside the kiln, where a fire was lit for slow, even drying.

A Celtic recipe for an ointment of elderflowers called for combining roughly 5 fl oz (140 ml) of oil in a pot (almond oil is used today) with an ounce (28 g) of lanolin. The pot was warmed over hot water until the melted oil and lanolin mixed, then elderflowers were added until they were just covered by the oil. The mixture was heated for about half an hour with gentle stirring, then strained while hot and a little honey added. This made a soothing skin cream that allayed irritation.

Simple but effective lotions were made using milk, buttermilk or whey, and sometimes cream. A handful of herbs was soaked in the milk or whey for two or three hours, then strained and a little honey added. After mixing thoroughly, a little ground oatmeal or bran was added. Meadowsweet, elderflowers or thyme were gently warmed in the liquid and left to infuse for a few hours, after which the lotion was strained and thickened with a little more oatmeal.

Honey for sweetening and lotions was prepared from the wild hive comb by warming the honeycomb in water, standing overnight, and then straining and filtering the liquor

through fine cloth. The strength of the honey solution was tested by putting a fresh egg in it: if the egg floated, the solution was fully concentrated. Among the sweet dishes prepared by the Celts were blancmanges, made by boiling Irish moss (the dried seaweed carrageen) in milk and adding bramble syrup and honey to sweeten.

The Celtic herbalist and wise woman used an opium-like drug obtained from the wild lettuce (*Lactuca virosa*) when wounds or other injuries were life-threatening. The alkaloid was obtained by slitting the stem of the plant and collecting the milky sap that exuded.

Only one poisonous grass remains in Britain, and it is becoming rare. This is Darnel, a species of rye grass, and every farmer since the Celtic Age had done his utmost to exclude it from the fields, where it grows among barley and other grain. If the seeds of Darnel are ingested, there is an intoxicating effect, followed by dizziness, delirium and loss of vision. If grain for bread-making is contaminated with Darnel seeds, similar symptoms arise. Some historians believe that Darnel was the weed referred to in the Gospel parable of the wheat and the tares. ⊕ ⊕ ⊕

RITUAL
AND BELIEF

Early Celtic Religion

All of the information we have from classical Greco-Roman writers, together with modern archaeological evidence, brings us no closer to unveiling the mystery of early Celtic religion. We can, of course, infer a whole range of tempting notions, but religion, at least among the early Celts, remains largely an enigma.

Celtic belief centred around a "god great", the supreme being, and a pantheon of gods and goddesses of lesser status. The spirit world (or Otherworld) existed side by side with the temporal world. Gods and goddesses, even mortals, were able to move between the two worlds almost at will. These beliefs would make the later Celts receptive to Christianity, which taught that the Son of God took human form and, after immense suffering at the Crucifixion, rose again and returned to His Father's house. Indeed, many miraculous accomplishments were recounted in Celtic myth and legend—wondrous tales of triumph over the forces of darkness, of immaculate conception and mystical power. The Celtic perception of the Otherworld is outlined in the tale "Echtrae Conli", in which the Irish king Cormac, alone on the ramparts of Tara, sees a stranger approach, finely

dressed and with the bearing of a warrior. Cormac asks the stranger, "From whence do you come"? He replies: "From a land where there is only truth, and there is no old age, nor decay, nor sadness, nor envy, nor jealousy, nor hatred, nor arrogance".

Evidently, the early Celts did not build roofed stone shrines, except for the unusual examples in Provence, France. Some temples may have been wooden-built, as at Fulford (Oxfordshire). Here we find a circular shrine of the Romano-Celtic era. Preceded by an Iron Age temple, it must have been a cult gathering place like those at Worth (Kent) and Muntham Court (Sussex). The latter was associated with a cult well and may have been a healing centre.

Most of our primary information on Celtic religion comes from inscriptions on altars of the Romano-Celtic period in continental Europe and Britain. Roman deities appear side by side with Celtic gods and goddesses, but the degree to which Celtic belief was influenced by Roman usage is not clear. Among the Celtic deities named are Belenus and Epona, the horse-goddess (the only Celtic goddess to be honoured in Rome). Lugh was known both on the Continent and in Britain, but no shrine has been found inscribed with his name. The mother goddesses (*Matres*

or *Matronae*) were more widespread: their cult dates back at least to Neolithic times.

Samhain (Gaelic, *Samhainn*) marked the beginning of the Celtic year and was celebrated on the night of October 31st (later observed as Hallowe'en, the vigil of All Hallows). At Samhain, the veil between the Otherworld and humankind was torn aside: the earth opened, spirits roamed the land, the warrior dead came back to life. Gods and demons walked the dark places, and the forest and bogland shook as their steps released the spirits of the Underworld. The air was filled with cries and lamentation; the incantations of ancient priests and Druids echoed to the night sky. This was the moment when the cycle of fertility was renewed, between the dark time of the year and the light of the new year to come. Fires were lit on the hilltops to guide returning warriors, and the *sídh* released phantoms and goblins to ride the night winds. In Dorset, local legend tells that a Stone-age horseman rides the road near an ancient burial mound. This road (between Cranborne and Handley) bisects the old Roman road to Sarum and is, indeed, an ancient trackway that linked the Celtic villages of the Durotriges with the coast. The description of the ghostly rider sounds like that of a Celtic youth— bare-legged and wrapped in a long grey cloak. Practitioners

of the rites continued to observe Samhain in the traditional way, but with the conversion of the British Isles to Christianity, it was transmuted into a harvest festival.

Three other seasonal festivals would eventually be incorporated into the Church calendar under new auspices. Imbolc was a fertility festival held on the first day of February and associated with the goddess Brigit. Beltane was kept on the first of May, when cattle were ritually purified by being driven between two fires. Household fires were extinguished and then rekindled with a torch lit at the ritual fire. Lughnasa was the agrarian harvest festival, celebrated for a month between mid-July and mid-August.

Cereal grain was the mainstay of daily life, and so highly regarded that ears of grain are depicted on Celtic coins and stone carvings. Ransoms for hostages were sometimes paid in grain, and laws levied certain fines in grain (they later formed part of the tithe system operative in most parishes). Sheaves of corn and barley are still displayed at Harvest Home and Church festivals, as are the traditional Corn-Dollie and Corn-Maiden, both made from the last cutting of grain. These straw figures were symbolic of fertility. At both sowing and harvest times they were carried around the fields in procession, signalling commencement of the harvest feast. ⊕ ⊕ ⊕

The Druids

Members of the Druid priesthood were trained for up to twenty years to serve as guardians of the mysteries of their religion. Their traditions were passed on orally, and they also served as tribal judges and historians. Their secret rites were carried out primarily in the densely wooded areas the Romans called "sacred groves".

Pliny the Elder, writing in the first century AD, left one of the very few accounts of Druid practices. He described them as wearing white robes as they celebrated the sixth night of the new moon by cutting a sprig of mistletoe from a sacred oak with a gold sickle. (The word Druid comes from the Gaelic for "knowing the oak tree".) The mistletoe was dropped onto a white cloak spread below the tree, and, according to Pliny, was used in magic potions. The Druids had a knowledge of astronomy equal to that of the Romans, and they practised a form of astrological prediction of future events. Their calendar was based on a year comprising twelve months of thirty days each, with extra days interspersed, similar to the Julian calendar.

In Druidic teaching, there was no "original sin" and no hereditary sin, thus no evasion of responsibility for one's own actions. Each family (kindred group) was held respon-

sible for the actions of all its members: thus the family group "policed" and punished wrongdoing by its own members. Failure to do so was a serious breach of Celtic law, for which the entire family group was punished.

Since the Druidic class was both a powerful religious force and a politically unifying influence among the Celts, Roman military authorities were instructed to do everything possible to uproot and destroy the Druids. In both Gaul and Britain, Druidic priests were made outcasts, and as a large proportion of Celtic chiefs were themselves Druids, their dissolution by Roman legions achieved both political and cultural aims. The Druids and their followers and lawmakers were killed or driven from their lands, their sanctuaries destroyed and the sacred groves put to the torch or the axe. Thus the Roman military tried to put an end to Celtic civilisation. ⊕ ⊕ ⊕

Celtic Sanctuaries

In the writings of Greek and Roman historians, we learn much about sacred sanctuaries of the Celt, often found near lakes or rivers, and in remote forest sites. The poet

Lucan describes one such sacred wood, and Caesar and other Roman generals destroyed such sanctuaries in both Gaul and Britain. They reflected the people's affinity with the natural world. The Celtic word *nemeton*, found in many place names, refers to sacred places in woods and remote areas. Lucan comments that the Druids dwelled in *nemora alta* (dense groves), and adds that "they worship their gods without making use of temples". Other sacred sanctuaries existed at the sources of rivers, including the Marne and the Seine where devotional wood carvings have been found. At Llyn Cerrig Bach (Anglesey), many artefacts were recovered in what had once been a lake—weapons, cauldrons and bronze items—comprising ritual offerings that ceased after the Romans plundered the island in AD 60, destroying the woods that Tacitus described as "devoted to barbarous superstition".

During Romano-Celtic times, probably through the influence of Roman practice, curses were inscribed on lead sheets, thrown into a spring or stream, or nailed to a post, frequently near a temple or shrine, to seek revenge against offenders. Excavations made at Uley (Gloucestershire) uncovered more than a hundred such curses. ⊕ ⊕ ⊕

The Celtic Christian Church

The precise date when Christianity first reached the British Isles remains a mystery. The Celts traded throughout Europe and the Mediterranean, and it is probable that merchants first brought word of the inspired prophets. News of the Risen Christ would have spread like wildfire through Celtic society. Indeed, many traditional stories suggest that the Celts were well prepared to receive this revelation. Phoenician and Aramaic traders brought news from the Holy Land. Legend relates that Joseph of Arimathea, the wealthy merchant who provided Christ's tomb, came to Cornwall to trade for tin, bringing the Child Jesus with him. According to the Acts of the Apostles, St. Paul addressed the Celts (Gauls) in Galatia.

The earliest Celtic Christians, called the Culdees, accepted the Old Latin (Itala) Bible as the revealed word of God—a theology to be accepted and obeyed in every particular, in the tradition of the Druidic "word". Speculation or debate concerning the revealed Word was forbidden. God was supreme provider and creator. Men and women were created by Him, and through the exercise of devotion and the ability to live according to God's Word it was possible to

enter into Paradise, the Land of the Ever Young. The notion of free will was the touchstone of sanctity.

The concept of the Trinity was coloured by Celtic tradition and belief. As in the Druidic teaching, there was no place for those who chose to disobey, a point on which the Culdee Church was adamant. Those who rebelled against God the Father could not dwell with Jesus in Paradise, the Land of the Ever Young. There was no provision for half-measures, deathbed repentances, or priestly absolution. Only the Trinity could forgive, and all were subject to that judgement and wisdom beyond human understanding. The doctrine of original sin was roundly rejected in what would be defined by Rome as the Pelagian heresy.

The Culdee faith drew together two strands of doctrinal belief: the Druidic teaching and the revealed word of God in the Biblical texts. But the Roman Church made every effort to stamp out what they called the pagan beliefs of the Celtic people and to destroy the Culdees. Celtic sanctuaries and burial places were desecrated and churches built above the ruins. The name Culdees (from *cele de*, servants of God) was probably derived from the name given to the Christianised Druids in Britain. Gaulish refugees found asylum among the western Celts, the Silures of Wales,

where they established a Druidic College and were hospitably received by the king Arvigarus. They were given twelve hides (or ploughs) of land which was free of taxation. The Domesday Survey of AD 1088 records that "The *Domus Dei* (House of God) in the great monastery of Glastonbury...possesses its own villa, XII hides of land which have never paid tax".

The Celtic Church survived as a cohesive entity in the British Isles until the Synod of Whitby in AD 664, when King Oswy, influenced by his queen, the daughter of Ethelbert, the Saxon king of Kent, resolved to adopt the Roman calendar date for Easter. From that time onward, the Culdees were more and more coerced into conforming to papal authority from Rome. Their ceremonial days were incorporated into the Church calendar in the belief that this would bring the "pagans" into the fold. This ambivalent attitude to the old beliefs lingers even in the present age. In recent years, a vicar of St. Stephens in Bury, Lancashire, banned the local "rose queens" because the tradition is "firmly rooted in pagan fertility rites, like dancing round the Maypole".

The Roman Church used its political influence to permeate the Saxon royal assemblies and outlaw the Culdees. It also claimed that many Culdee saints were supporters of

the Roman Church, despite the fact that these saints had struggled against the Roman faith all their lives. St. Patrick (b. 636), for example, was a Culdee, but has been depicted as an ardent follower of the Roman faith despite his Druidic background. He revived the Christian faith initially brought to Ireland before AD 61.

The old tales of Celtic barbarity, sacrificial rites and half-naked savagery, a legacy of Greek and Roman writers, were revived among the Saxon nobility (sassenachs). So successful was this policy of denigration that it gained uncritical belief through repetition. In fact, it formed the substance of Celtic "history" taught in classrooms down to the twentieth century. Recent archaeological discoveries and new research have done much to redress these revisionist histories, and it is hoped that this book and others like it will provide a more accurate and balanced view of our Celtic heritage. ⊕ ⊕ ⊕

Legends and Folk Beliefs

Tales of Otherworld spirits, spectres and faery folk abound in Celtic myth and legend, but as a result of the near-extinction of the Celtic tongue, and the vast depopulation of the crofts and smallholdings, few of these survive from what must have been a great store of folklore and heroic saga. Tales associated with the magical world of the *sídh* (prehistoric burial mounds) are rife and bear a striking relationship. They centre on a mysterious door on the side of the *sídh*. Inside is a supernatural world populated by gods, demons, or even beautiful fair-haired spirits who wait for humans to join them at their revels. Usually, the inhabitants of the *sídh* mound are the spirit-folk of past ages, highly skilled in the magical arts and willing to take a part in human affairs.

The mysterious mounds relate indirectly, but significantly, to *The Book of Invasions* (*Lebor Gabála*). Here we learn of the various bands of warlike tribes that fought over and colonised Ireland. First came an invasion from Spain, but its members perished in a plague. Then came the Fir Bolg, with the Fir Domnann and Fir Galioin. These were followed by the Tuatha De Danann (the people of the goddess Danu), who

conquered both the Fir Bolg and the Fomori in great bat-
tles and took possession of the land. Later, the Tuatha De
Danann (who became Celtic gods) were defeated by the
Milesians, who advanced on Tara, the seat of kingship, and
defeated the Tuatha after a heroic struggle. Most of the
Tuatha left Ireland, but some of their gods remained, including the Dagda (father of gods). All had to leave their dwelling
and live out their magical lives in the *sídh*. In the Boyne
Valley are the *tumuli* of the ancient dead, where Aengus Oc,
the Dagda's son, dwells.

Many stories and folk tales have been woven around the
sídh or fairy-mound, such as the story of Aengus Oc's dream
of a beautiful girl, for love of whom he falls into a wasting
sickness. His parents, Boann, goddess of the Boyne, and
the Dagda, try in vain to find the girl. Finally, the Bodb, who
lives in the *sídh* at Munster, learns that she is the daughter of Ethal Anbhuail of the *sídh* in Connaught. The Dagda
and several companions visit Ethal Anbhuail, and he is
forced to tell how his daughter may be found and give his
opinion on how Aengus may win her love.

A few centuries ago almost every object had its connec-
tion with goblins or spirits, and every action of man or beast
had some supernatural significance. Spilling salt was an ill

omen; if one's head itched, it was a sign of rain; toothache meant that your loved one was unfaithful. A white speck on the fingernail was the sign of a forthcoming gift. A candle that burned with a blue flame was a sign that spirits were near, and when the tallow ran down the side of the candle at a wake, he who was sitting nearest would be doomed to suffer some disaster.

The superstition that prohibits having thirteen people at the table derives from the way Celtic chiefs rode into battle. With his bearers and shieldmen, the chief had three warriors before him, two at either hand, and three behind. These together with the chariot bearers and himself numbered twelve. The thirteenth rider who accompanied them was Death, the unseen companion of chieftain and warrior alike.

"Touching wood" is said to derive from a Christian belief, but this was an adaptation. Gods and spirits inhabited trees, and the Druidic cult worship of trees had an important part in Celtic mysteries. Some place names contain the word eburos, for the yew, one of the most revered trees. The ash, rowan (mountain ash) and oak were also sacred.

The owl's screech outside a cottage meant that a death would follow; where there was sickness, the number of times the owl called denoted the days remaining before

death. Stones found with a hole through them were called "witches' stones", and farmers frequently put them into their byres to protect cattle from witches. Lead miners would sometimes wear such a stone around their necks on a piece of cord. The efficacy of the stone was certain if it came from a stream near a witches' domain. A rowan tree beside the door was a sure means of protection from witches, and a piece of rowan wood carried about the person counteracted their bane and ensured good fortune. The piece of rowan had to be cut with a new knife from a tree previously unknown to the seeker. To protect young lambs and calves from the spells of the witch, collars of rowan were placed about their necks.

Mermaids were not the only sea-folk to figure in Celtic stories: sea-witches abounded along the desolate and rocky coasts of the northlands, and there were occasional reports that a merman had been captured by a fisherman. In one such story, the merman was taken to a cottage, treated kindly and fed upon raw fish. The merman was courteous and well disposed, but after a few weeks he became restless and homesick. One day he stole quietly out of the cottage and made his way to the sea, but he did not depart immediately. He waited until his human friends arrived at

the shore and called out his thanks before he bade them farewell and dived into the sea, to be seen no more.

Not until the mid-1700s was there written mention of "the hungry grass". It was a well-known phenomenon in parts of Ireland and the Highlands, especially on the high hills and among the peat mosses where the sheep grazed. The hungry grass is described as a coarse grass that appears in autumn. Whitish in colour, it is often found beside sheep-walks. If an unwary traveller steps on the hungry grass, which is known as *féar gorta* in western Ireland, a sensation of great hunger and prostration overwhelms him immediately. The victim collapses and unless some food is taken at once—the smallest morsel of bread will suffice—death follows rapidly. No one walks the hills without a piece of bread in his pocket. Poet Donagh MacDonagh wrote of *féar gorta*:

Crossing the shallow holdings high above sea
Where few birds nest, the luckless foot may pass
From the bright safety of experience
Into the terror of the hungry grass.

⊕ ⊕ ⊕

Marriage Rites

A mong the common people, the marriage ceremony was a simple ritual for centuries. It consisted of little more than a declaration by the couple before the assembled villagers that they were man and wife. This declaration was often made beside a menhir, or standing stone, which had a hole through its centre, and the two parties would clasp hands through the hole and declare themselves a married couple. This form of ceremony, called "handfasting" in the Highlands, constituted a legal marriage by declaration until it was finally invalidated by Scotland's 1939 Marriage Act.

The ancient ritual of offering foot baths to arriving guests was carried on as a Scottish wedding custom up until recent times. The night before the wedding (whether handfasting before witnesses or a church ceremony), the ritual of foot washing took place at both the bride's and the groom's family homes. A silver coin was put into the basin, and after the little ceremony was completed, the unmarried guests competed for possession of the coin, as it was thought that the one who obtained it would be the next to marry. ⊕ ⊕ ⊕

funeral Rites and the Otherworld

G raves richly furnished with goods indicate Celtic belief in the afterlife or Otherworld, described in so many legends. But this belief was not necessarily similar to that of, say, the ancient Egyptians. The Celts conceived of the Otherworld as a place outside the time-space continuum and death as no more than a brief pause in the cycle of rebirth. Certainly, the rich trappings that decorated many burial chambers denoted respect, and perhaps ostentation on the part of rich and powerful families, but death was to them no more than a brief interlude before the magical process of transmutation.

Peat-preserved bodies found in Celtic bogs, including Tollund-man and Lindow-man, have been identified by some archaeologists as sacrificial victims, but they may have been criminals executed for crimes against the community. There is no absolute evidence that human sacrifice was practised by the Celts as part of religious ritual. Accounts of such sacrifices by classical writers may well have been simply deliberate sensationalism, and reference to such gruesome ritual no more than an attempt to defame the "barbarian" tribes. Similarly, the so-called cult of the head—the practice of pre-

serving the heads of vanquished enemies—was related to the Celtic belief in eternal life: the head was considered the abode of the soul. Many of the saints who brought Christianity to the British Isles were beheaded by hostile Celts or Picts as a way of testing the supernatural power of the missionaries. If they were of divine origin, they should be able to restore their heads to their bodies.

The Celtic Otherworld was a fabulous country where gentle streams meandered through green countryside on an endless summer afternoon; where birds sang, music played and the happy dweller rested on a grassy knoll. There was honey and mead and laughter, no sense of the passing of time, no sin and no guilt. People were unblemished, with snow-white skin and golden hair. They wore raiment of spun silver and gold; rich chains hung about their waists and shoulders, jewelled bands about their brows. Sweet new milk and honey, ale and wine filled silver drinking bowls. This was the *Tir nan n'Og* of the Celt, Land of the Ever Young, where the warrior dined in the Hall of Silver Pillars with companions so beautiful that no other earthly joy excelled the pleasures of the feasting hall.

Originally, Celtic peoples cremated their dead. Later, they were buried in various ways, from the Neolithic barrow

mound or *sídh* to the post-Christian consecrated ground. The traditional wake does not survive in Britain, and in Ireland the custom is disappearing. In past times, a body was waked for at least two nights, sometimes three. Women paid their respects only during the day: the wake was an all-male affair, each person having his allotted part to play. One participant would be responsible for speaking well of the dead, another for naming the family and antecedents and their history. Others had the tasks of handing out pipes and tobacco, distributing whisky and porter, and organising the wake games. Some games were simply tests of strength and skill, others were party tricks, but all were generated by ancient Celtic belief, which had a deep reverence for memory. It was customary for the bards to eulogise the valorous deeds, skills and culture of the deceased, the *filid* (or sayer) giving an account of his or her ancestry. To this day, people of Celtic heritage are known as powerful speakers and storytellers. Their reverence for the spoken word communicates itself through oral history, humour, liturgy and eulogy. ⊕ ⊕ ⊕

Map of the British Isles

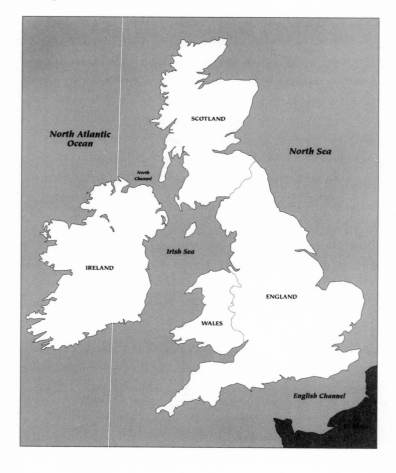

Principal Celtic Tribes of the British Isles in AD 43

The Belgae	Southern England
The Cantii	Kent
The Trinovantes	Essex
The Iceni	East Anglia
The Brigantes Confederation	Northern England
The Parisii	East Yorkshire
The Coritani	Central England
The Cornovi	Central England
The Dobunni	Central England
The Ordovices	Wales
The Silures	Wales
The Caledonians (ancestors of the Picts)	Scotland

Glossary of Celtic Words and Phrases

bardh	poet, composer and singer
brothas	porridge
carrageen	a purplish, edible seaweed, also called Irish moss
cele de	servants of God; origin of "Culdee" Christian Church
coirce	oat
curad-mir	the champion's portion of meat
fillid	storyteller
korma	beer made from barley
laver	a bright-green, edible seaweed, also called sea-lettuce
petia	peat
plaide	blanket
poitin	potheen, an Irish whisky
salaan	salt
seite	animal-like
sídh	ancient burial mound
skean dhu	black knife
sporan	leather pouch or purse
tuath	tribe, kinship group

INDEX